Worship
and
Remembrance

•

Volume II

Author of:
> *Nosu Nuggets (Missionary)* *
> *Be Ye Holy* *
> *Consuming Fires* *
> *The House of God* *
> *Missionary in the Orient*
> *The Gospel of His Grace*
> *Seers of Israel*
> *Worship and Remembrance*

*Now out of print

Meditations on the Lord's Supper

Worship
and
Remembrance

Volume II

by
DANIEL SMITH

Copies available from
DANIEL SMITH
2803 West 14th Avenue
Vancouver 8 B.C., Canada V6K 2X3

Printed in the United States of America

CONTENTS

3

Contents   5

PREFACE

My first book of meditations on the Lord's Supper, entitled *Worship and Remembrance*, and comprised of forty-four such meditations, has proved a real blessing to those who seek to worship God "in spirit and in truth," and who have great appreciation of the substitutionary sacrifice made by our Lord Jesus Christ on Calvary's cross.

Many and sweet have been the testimonies sent me that precious souls were nurtured by the messages and hymn quotations. Within two years 5,000 copies in two editions were dispersed, mostly sold privately while I was conducting meetings, and quite a number by written requests for the book.

We servants of the Lord, set apart by Him for the work of the ministry, live and rejoice when the Lord's people, for whose spiritual good we watch and labor, enter into the full faith of the gospel, exercise themselves in worship before the Lord God, and fill their hearts with rapturous, adoring praise of Him whose abounding love has redeemed us.

It is my prayer, in sending forth this new series of fifty messages, that this also shall minister to your spiritual welfare, and that the Holy Spirit will work mightily and mercifully in your heart to make these things real to you. If this proves to be so, then I shall count my labor in writing the book light indeed, and my prayers all too few.

I thank God that through this humble means I have this touch upon your life and this access to your home. It is my friendly whisper to your heart of the very essence of divine truth and revelation, and a kindly directing of your eye to Him who is "fairer than the children of men" (Psalm 45:2), and who alone is worthy of your worship, praise, and adoration forever.

My gratitude is again extended to my two friends, Mrs. Eileen Firth and Bertram Shelton, for scanning the manuscript and making necessary adjustments. The hymns quoted are almost all from the hymnbooks currently used in our assembly worship meetings. My daughter Roxie, now of Arlington, Washington, has again come to my aid with her work in typing the manuscript.

Your ministering servant,

DANIEL SMITH

WORSHIP—SYMBOLIC OR SPIRITUAL

The hour cometh, and now is, when the true worship-
pers shall worship the Father in spirit and in truth: for the
Father seeketh such to worship Him (John 4:23).

The reason for writing the Epistle to the Hebrews was to convince those Hebrews professing faith in the Lord Jesus that the ritualistic and ceremonial ways of approaching God had passed away. The ritualistic form of things was a grand spectacular with its beautiful temple, gorgeous robes, priests and sacrifices, singers and choirs.

All such contributed to the grand spectacle. It was a God-ordained system for that particular dispensation. It was full of color and music, heavy with incense, a sight fascinating to the senses. It was hard for the Hebrews to believe that all that had passed away, that the Lord had forsaken the Temple in Jerusalem, that He no longer regarded Jewish priests and sacrifices, that the institutions of Moses had lost their utility and usefulness.

The Ritualistic Worship

This ritualisitc and symbolic form of worship was that which the woman of Samaria referred to as she conversed with our Lord at the well of Sychar. "Our fathers worshipped in this mountain; and ye say, that in Jerusalem is the place where men ought to worship" (John 4:20).

She may have been evading a conscience awakened to her sinful life, but she was also genuinely groping for the true meaning of worship. She knew a form of worship—a form "in

9

this mountain" and another form "at Jerusalem." In both places there was that which was related to God's appointed way to approach Him in that dispensation. That form had its temples, its priests, its sacrifices, its altars, its incense, its vestments. When the woman said, "Our fathers worshipped in this mountain" (Mount Gerizim), she may have been referring to Abraham and Jacob, both of whom erected altars in Samaria.

Thus both in Samaria and in Jerusalem there was that which was known as worship. In this worship there was recognition of the true and living God, that He was worthy of worship, and that such worship could only be offered through the priests and sacrifices appointed by God. The priests were His ministers—His altar servants—especially set apart to serve Him and His people. It was all a very precious rite, and it was all symbolic of the Saviour's worth. It taught how His shed blood was necessary to approach God. The altar taught the bleeding cross. The shed blood taught the wholeness of the atoning sacrifice.

The Spiritual Worship

The Lord Jesus then said to the woman, "Woman, believe Me, the hour cometh, when ye shall neither in this mountain, nor yet at Jerusalem, worship the Father. . . . But the hour cometh, and now is, when the true worshippers shall worship the Father in spirit and in truth: for the Father seeketh such to worship Him. God is a Spirit: and they that worship Him must worship Him in spirit and in truth" (John 4:21,23-24).

The hour for true worship had come. The symbolic worship thus ended. It was done away. He to whom all symbols pointed had now come. Believers, then, must look to Him. They had seen animal victims without number die. Each drop of blood from those sacrifices pointed forward to the Lamb of God. They had their witnessing priests who spared not the innocent animals but struck the death blow to them. The blazing fires on the altars witnessed the consuming of their prey. His people were shown in symbol that in sacrifice all demands of wrath were met.

But when the Son of God hung on a curse-bearing tree, reality was set before them. Guilt was taken away, and sinners were ransomed by the Lord's anguish. The hour had come. The shadows and symbols had passed. The hour had struck for the reality of worship.

This was a new worship—not ceremonial, but spiritual. The new worship was true worship. And the Lord Jesus told the woman of Samaria three times that true worship was the worship of the Father. The Father sought such worshipers. From the cross onward there was to be an age when the Father would seek true worshipers.

No such name for God had ever been given Israel. He was to them Elohim, the God of power; El Shaddai, the God of provision; Jehovah, the God of promise; El Elyon, the God of preservation—but never Father. The approach to God as Father, and the worship of Him as Father, only became possible through the coming of His Son, the completion of the redemptive sacrifice, and the impartation of the Holy Spirit, who would enable true worship. This kind of worship stands in contrast to what was of old in Israel—a worship which at best was incomplete and in shadow.

May we, then, worship the Son through the enabling of the indwelling Spirit? Yes, we may! The Father Himself has said, "All men should honour the Son, even as they honour the Father" (John 5:23). For further verification of this, we are given a view of Heaven in Revelation 5, where both the Father and the Son are joint objects of worship. "Blessing, and honour, and glory, and power, be unto Him that sitteth upon the throne, and unto the Lamb for ever and ever" (Revelation 5:13). The Lamb, who was slain, shares the worship due only to God, because He is God—God the Son.

> Father, we worship Thee,
> Thro' Thy beloved Son;
> And, by the Spirit, now draw near
> Before Thy holy throne.

We bless Thee Thou art love,
  How vast that matchless grace,
Whose breadth and length and height and depth
  No finite mind can trace.

For what Thou art, we praise,
  And worship, and adore:
To Father, Son, and Spirit be
  The glory evermore!

ALFRED P. GIBBS

WORSHIP THROUGH OUR LORD'S PRIESTHOOD

Wherefore, holy brethren, partakers of the heavenly
calling, consider the . . . High Priest of our profession, Christ
Jesus (Hebrews 3:1).

Worship of the living God is possible only through a high
priest. This was true in the Old Testament times of symbolic
rites—the childhood period of human history. In the past,
Aaron and his sons were chosen and consecrated to that office
(Leviticus 8:22-23). In the spiritual worship of this present
age—that is, worship in the Spirit and by the Spirit—we all
have boldness to enter into the very presence of God because
of our High Priest, Christ Jesus, and His completed work.

The main lesson of the Old Testament is Christ, set forth
in types. Thus the priesthood of Aaron has much to teach us
both by comparison and by contrast. It casts light and luster
on our Lord's office, which is the heart-blood of all God-given
symbolism. The Aaronic symbols such as the sanctuary, the

altar, the priests, the vestments, the sacrifices, all have been done away. What we have now is the reality of these things. All is in Christ, the fulfillment of all types and symbols. This teaching concerning the priesthood is spoken of as the strong meat of the Word, which produces spiritual maturity (Hebrews 5:11-14). It is therefore most important.

Worship Through the Jewish Priesthood

The Jewish high priest was chosen from among men. His work was to "offer both gifts and sacrifices for sins" to God on behalf of the people (Hebrews 5:1). The most important day in the life of the nation of Israel was the day of atonement. Aaron was first to slay the sin offering and with the blood of it to enter into the holiest. There he put sweet incense on the coals of fire taken from the altar. The resultant clouds of incense hid the glory of God "that he die not."

He then sprinkled the blood of the sin offering on the ark, making a propitiation before God for his own and his people's sins. Finally he came out, confessed the sins of his people, and transferred them, by the laying on of hands, to the live goat, which bore them away where they could never be found.

The qualifications for this office were: (1) that he have the grace of patience, so as to have "compassion on the ignorant"; (2) that he have a sense of human weakness, so as to understand the trials of his people; and (3) that he comprehend his own sin, so as not to become proud in his office and despise God's people (Hebrews 5:2-3).

No man was allowed to take to himself the honor of the priesthood, but he who was chosen of God (Hebrews 5:4). It was necessary that blood be shed for sin; but, before forgiveness could be obtained, the high priest had to carry that shed blood within the veil and present it before God.

One of the most interesting points in the matter of the high priest's vestments was the ephod. Attached to it were the shoulder stones and breastplate on which were engraved the names of the children of Israel. The ephod was made of threads of gold and also of ordinary spun threads of blue,

purple, and scarlet, on a white background (Exodus 39:3), all
of which are a rich garden of delight in pointing out features
of Christ Jesus our Lord in His Person, and in His office as
High Priest on behalf of His redeemed people.

Worship Through Christ's High Priesthood

"So also Christ"—that is, He was chosen of God. He did
not grasp for this honor. The Father conferred it (John 8:54).
Unlike the Jewish high priests, He had no sin of His own to
atone for, being the Son of God. He, being very God of very
God, and true and perfect Man, is seen in the construction of
the robe of the ephod. The gold of it signified the divine
nature (Hebrews 1:8)—there being divine Sonship in His deity
which was eternally pre-existent to His incarnation—and the
ordinary spun threads spoke of His true manhood.

The prime qualification of our Lord was that He was
"touched with the feeling of our infirmities" (Hebrews 4:15).
This does not imply any weakness, but rather that in His
earthly life He experienced all emergent human conditions:
humble birth, poor environment, hunger, thirst, temptation,
the care for a widow and children (since Joseph died early).
In His public ministry He experienced homelessness, treachery
of foes, desertion by friends, lack of understanding, and an
early death. All these experiences were designed to make Him
an understanding and sympathetic High Priest.

His high priesthood was different to that of Aaron's.
Jewish high priests could serve only for a limited period.
Death interrupted their continuance. Nor could they ever sit
down in their service in token of work accomplished. They
always stood, for their work was never finished. There was no
seat in the holiest for any Jewish high priest. He dared not sit.
Also, the sacrifice of animal blood could never take away sins,
but could only symbolically cover them until Christ came to
make the perfect sacrifice.

Our Lord was never an Aaronic priest. He could not be
a priest on earth of that order since He was of Judah and not
of Levi, the priestly tribe.

It was necessary, therefore, that another priesthood should come into view. This was shown even before the Levitical priesthood came into being. It came in view in Melchizedek (Genesis 14) who was "Without father, without mother, without descent, having neither beginning of days, nor end of life; but made like unto the Son of God; abideth a priest continually" (Hebrews 7:1-3). Thus our Lord was "a priest for ever after the order of Melchizedek" (Hebrews 7:17).

In His resurrection our Lord ascended into the true tabernacle above and entered with His own precious blood which "cleanseth from all sin." So He began in Heaven the high priestly ministry of His redeemed people, and became "the author of eternal salvation," since He continues forever after the power of an endless life and has an unchangeable priesthood. Therefore He is able to save to the uttermost of time (Hebrews 7:25-27).

It is because of His superior priesthood that we who believe may now draw near with boldness and do what none of the people of Israel dared to do: enter into the holiest of all (Hebrews 10:19-22). It is there that Jesus our Lord sits on the throne with the Father, having finished once and for all, and forever, the work of our redemption. Thus we may come and worship (Hebrews 9:26,28; 10:10,12,14).

> With joy we meditate the grace
>   Of our High Priest above;
> His heart is filled with tenderness,
>   His very name is Love.
>
> Touched with a sympathy within,
>   He knows our feeble frame:
> He knows what sorest trials mean,
>   For He has felt the same!
>
> But spotless, undefiled, and pure,
>   Our great Redeemer stood
> No stain of sin did e'er defile
>   The holy Lamb of God.

                    ISAAC WATTS

THE PRIESTHOOD OF BELIEVERS IN WORSHIP

> Let us draw near with a true heart in full assurance of
> faith, having our hearts sprinkled from an evil conscience,
> and our bodies washed with pure water (Hebrews 10:22).

> To whom coming . . . Ye also, as lively stones, are built
> up a spiritual house, an holy priesthood (1 Peter 2:4-5).

There is nothing about which there is more confusion
than this matter of priesthood. We surely need the Spirit of
God to unravel us from all the entanglements of men. We have
seen that the cross removes sin, and that the living God implants the living seed of a righteous life within us. We have been
translated into the kingdom of God's dear Son—a haven of
unruffled calm. We were once in transgression, but our Lord
has cleansed us from every stain. We now draw nigh to God
within the holiest, and do so to exercise a priestly ministry
before God.

Meaning of the Priesthood

The reality of spiritual things in the New Testament is
found in the pattern of the Old. There we see that priests were
made such by birth, and that their function was to offer "to
God . . . both gifts and sacrifices for sins" (Hebrews 5:1). The
Levites separated themselves from evil and went forth out of
the camp at Moses' call.

For this they were made into a priestly tribe, which God
had intended all His people to be (Exodus 19:6). Thus the
lives of the Levites were spent in nearness to God, and they
presented to God what was pleasing to Him. Provision was

16

made in the sacrifices for those who thus ministered before God. They ate of the selfsame victim in which God had so great satisfaction.

Here, then, we see in the realities of the New Testament that those only are priests who are thus born—born of God—who give themselves wholly to the Lord and have their all in Him. Their refreshment, health, and vigor flow from feeding upon Christ and His sacrifice. Those who have not separated themselves from evil cannot approach God, but only those who know forgiveness through the death of Christ, the God-chosen sacrifice, and who have their transgressions transferred to Him and borne by Him. All such believers are priests unto God as 1 Peter 2:5 makes very clear.

The Functions of the Priesthood

We have seen that the true believer in the Lord Jesus has liberty and boldness to approach God. But there are differing degrees of approach, as the Old Testament makes evident. There were three compartments in the Tabernacle, thus three degrees of approach. There were some who were ever in "the outer court"; then a chosen few who went into "the holy place"; then one who went into "the holiest of all." Through our Lord Jesus Christ and His finished work, believers now have boldness to enter into the holiest of all in the heavenlies, not as servants, not as friends, but as dear children. They may now speak to God on the throne of His glory without restraint—the liberty of a child in the fond presence of his father.

Here, before God, the function of His priestly ones is to offer sacrifices. It is not the presentation of our bodies for service, as in Romans 12:1; nor is it primarily for prayer or intercession. Because such believers have come to Him by God's prescribed way, they are qualified to offer spiritual sacrifices.

That way to God is described in a threefold manner. It is (1) a new and living way which was not opened as yet in Old Testament times, and thus you will notice the absence of any endearing language in addressing God; (2) it is "consecrated for us"—trodden first by the sacred feet of our Saviour, the Son of God, so that we may approach and address God as Father; and (3) it is "through the veil, that is . . . His flesh"—rent on Calvary's cross, and so opening the way for God's glory to shine out, and believing man to go in (Hebrews 10:19-20).

The house, which believers are, is a spiritual house. I am writing this after a visit to the vastly expensive and magnificent university in Tulsa, Oklahoma, built by a religious leader. The buildings, which are full of symbolism, are beautiful and imposing edifices costing many millions of dollars. One such is the very plush chapel called Christ's Chapel. But this kind of thing is not for this age. God's house is a spiritual entity of living believers. And the offerings of the Lord's priests are not material, but spiritual.

Here we part company, then, with all symbolism, and all ritualistic worship as in the Roman mass—a dreadful error. With those who are the Lord's people there must be no emphasis on magnificent buildings but rather on spiritual life. When we come before the Lord, we are in the realm of the spiritual and unseen, and not in the realm of what is material and visible. If we close our eyes in worship, it is only to help us shut out that realm of material and visible things.

Since the sacrifices to be offered are now spiritual, we are not to come with special and gorgeous vestments, or with incense, or altars, or crucifixes, or holy water, or bodily postures. These belong to this material world, whereas our approach is as a spiritual people in a spiritual realm.

And what are the sacrifices which we are to offer? What delights God? Nothing except the different aspects of His beloved Son. One time we present this about Him and His work; another time it is that about Him and His work. But all is an offering of Christ. It is this which ravishes God's heart, and ours. The substance of true worship is to offer to the Father in the power of the Holy Spirit the different facets of our Lord's Person and sacrifice when He offered Himself to God.

There are differing grades of such offerings to God. You will notice in the burnt offering of Leviticus 1, that some brought "of the herd" a bullock; some, a sheep; some, a fowl; some, turtledoves or young pigeons (Leviticus 1:3,10, 13,14). These may well represent differing grades of apprehension of Christ, of heart devotion to the Lord God. Oh, how much do we bring of Christ to God?

> Through Thy precious body broken
>   Inside the veil;
> O what words to sinners spoken
>   Inside the veil!
> Precious as the blood that bought us,
>   Perfect as the love that sought us,
> Holy as the Lamb that brought us
>   Inside the veil.
>
> Lamb of God, through Thee we enter
>   Inside the veil!
> Cleansed by Thee, we boldly venture
>   Inside the veil:
> Not a stain; a new creation;
>   Ours is such a full salvation;
> Low we bow in adoration
>   Inside the veil.

ELIZABETH DARK

JOY IN WORSHIP

Enter into His gates with thanksgiving, and into His courts with praise: be thankful unto Him, and bless His name (Psalm 100:4).

I will joy in the God of my salvation (Habakkuk 3:18).

Those of us who have traveled in foreign lands have been shocked at the lewd, licentious abominations men worship. In God's calling Israel to be a vessel for His own revealings, we see how different was their worship to that of the nations around.

Israel was called to worship the living God "in the beauty of holiness." Each mercy from God brought forth the louder praise. Gratitude expanded their adoration. As God's goodness fell in swelling showers, so the heat of devotion ascended in higher flame. David, in the psalms of worship, rises to great heights of exuberant joy before the Lord. He soars high on the wings of adoring praise to God's holy name.

It was never intended that worship be morose, and the skies over the head of a worshiping people be full of somber gloom. David even danced with joy before the Lord (2 Samuel 6:14). Worship was robust, not anemic; virile, not lifeless; spontaneous, not forced. There was a natural overflowingness of the heart in worship. "O come, let us sing unto the LORD: let us make a joyful noise to the rock of our salvation" (Psalm 95:1).

Joy in Going up to God's House

It ought always to be a joy to anticipate worship, to go where the Lord is in the midst. It is surely the full grant of blessedness to meet the Lord, the living God, and our Saviour. In Old Testament times this was expressed in Israel as "going up to mount Zion."

It was so different from Sinai. It was at Sinai they heard the law. It spelled out God's will, what must be if they would be accepted of Him. "This do!" and life is purchased—Heaven is won. If man shares God's holiness, then he may ascend God's throne. But man failed, and hope from self died forever. The broken law frowns terribly upon men. It claims its payment. It utters its inexorable curse. Perfect obedience is its due. One breach makes it a foe forever.

But Zion's mount is in the Promised Land, and symbolizes God's system of grace. It is bathed in perpetual sunshine. It calls men to come and meet with God. "All your males shall appear before Me in Zion"—and three times a year they came! "The joy of the whole earth, is mount Zion" (Psalm 48:2). Zion means "projection." It was in the world, but rose out of the world and jutted high into the heavenlies. It represented a heavenly position, a heavenly consciousness, a heavenly hope, a heavenly education, and a heavenly joy.

As they climbed Zion's mountain, the Israelites sang Psalms 120 through 134. These are called "psalms of degrees" or "of ascent." On the earthly level Israel was a divided and scattered people, but Zion drew them together. The higher they climbed, the nearer they came to one another, until, on the top, they were together and sang: "Behold, how good and how pleasant it is for brethren to dwell together in unity!" (Psalm 133:1)

Unity is not a mere organizational thing. It is the outcome of spiritual ascent into our heavenly things in Christ. And the higher and higher these people climbed mount Zion with God's house in view, the louder and louder sounded their praises.

This response to God, and their ascent of Zion, was a most joyful experience. "O send out Thy light and Thy truth: let them lead me; let them bring me unto Thy holy hill, and to Thy tabernacles. Then will I go unto the altar of God, unto God my exceeding joy" (Psalm 43:3-4). If Israel had such joy in going up to Zion's hill to the house of the Lord, surely we believers of this dispensation have greater reason for joy in going to meet our Lord and our God.

Joy in God's Holy Presence

The last psalm in that special group of psalms is 134, and this they sang when on top of the mount and in God's house—in His holy presence. "Behold, bless ye the LORD, all ye servants of the LORD." No longer were their hearts cold, dead, rank with nature's weeds. They were now warm; faith sprang to life in them—they were in the house of God to adore and praise the beauties of the Lord. It was a grand reality of joy and bliss. What a lively, happy feeling it is to be where God's presence is real and manifested and realized.

We read that in those days: "It came even to pass, as the trumpeters and singers were as one, to make one sound to be heard in praising and thanking the LORD; and when they lifted up their voice with the trumpets and cymbals and instruments of music, and praised the LORD, saying, For He is good; for His mercy endureth for ever: that then the house was filled with a cloud, even the house of the LORD . . . for the glory of the LORD had filled the house of God" (2 Chronicles 5:13,14). Exultant souls brought down the glory of the Lord. It was an unfathomable flood of bliss.

We live in an era when God is known and worshiped as the Father of all who believe. Believers in the finished work of Christ Jesus are in a closer, more intimate, and more settled relationship with Him on the ground of redemption than Old Testament saints. The Holy Spirit has been given, the fruit of His life is joy, and His enabling help is the power for worship. What a joyous experience it should be, then, to be within the veil, in the presence of God, accepted of Him, made complete in Christ, all fully saved! Where are words to testify the joy of faith? The Spirit pauses and exclaims: "Unspeakable" (1 Peter 1:8). The Lord Himself is the believer's overflowing cup. We have access to His smile. The weary rest upon His loving breast. The full heart can throb no happier throb, know no greater joy, than pure, joyous worship of the Father and the Son.

> O for a thousand tongues to sing
>   My great Redeemer's praise,
> The glories of my God and King,
>   The triumphs of His grace.
>
> Jesus! the name that charms our fears,
>   That bids our sorrows cease;
> 'Tis music in the sinner's ears,
>   'Tis life, and health, and peace.
>
> Hear Him, ye deaf; His praise, ye dumb,
>   Your loosened tongues employ;
> Ye blind, behold your Saviour come;
>   And leap, ye lame, for joy.
>
>   CHARLES WESLEY

THE PLACE OF THE HOLY SPIRIT IN WORSHIP

They that worship Him [the Father] must worship Him
in spirit (John 4:24).

Worship by the Spirit (Philippians 3:3 RV).

The true objects of worship are the Father and the Son.
In His conversation with the woman of Samaria, the Lord made
clear what spiritual worship was. It was no longer a symbolic
rite, a ceremonial performance, but the worship of the Father.
All symbolism was done away with the coming of God's
beloved Son.

The hour had come for true worship. And the honor due
the Father was also to be given the Son—"That all men should
honour the Son, even as they honour the Father" (John 5:23).
The Lord Jesus was given worship and received worship from
men (John 9:38); from angels (Hebrews 1:6); and from all the
vast multitude of those in Heaven (Revelation 5:13-14). But
where does the Holy Spirit come in true worship? Is there no
place for Him, who is God the Spirit?

Worship in the Spirit

In talking with the woman at the well of Sychar about
worship, the Lord set true worship over against what was done
as worship in Samaria and at Jerusalem. It is important to
notice the words, "neither . . . nor . . . but" in John 4:21-23.
There was to be a change of location. No longer was it to be
a Samaritan worship in Samaria, or a Jewish worship at
Jerusalem, but the hour had come when worship would be an

utterly spiritual exercise. True worship would rise from the
spirits of redeemed men and women—and from them only,
because the Holy Spirit had given them new birth, a new life
in which was the faculty of, and ability for, worship.

The Jews were never true worshipers. They had a form
of worship and, with that form, dreamed life was safe—that
life was pleasing to God and that theirs was no polluted walk
as with the heathen; that God looked on them with no angry
frown; that death would land them on the shores of bliss; that
Heaven would be their home at last. But the prophets cut
through this delusion, and cried that God had no pleasure in
their sacrifices and worship. The Word of God through the
prophets cut down that carnal confidence, and showed them
that mere ceremonial worship still left them unclean, and still
without access to God's holy presence.

But "the hour cometh," said our Lord—that is, the hour
of His passion and, with His death, redemption work would
be finished. After His resurrection and ascension, the Lord
spread His hands, and poured down the promised Spirit.
Cloven tongues of fire fell and blazed on the heads of the as-
sembled company. They were all baptized in the Spirit, and
now all things were wrought in the Spirit. The location of
spiritual worship was now neither in Samaria, nor yet at Jerusalem, but in the spirits of redeemed men and women.

The reason given by our Lord is that "God is a Spirit," and the worship of men's hearts must answer to the
nature of God. "That which is born of the Spirit is spirit,"
and the exercises of the spirit do not belong to the material part of man. That is why there is no emphasis in the
New Testament on bodily postures or special dress. We
are not to imitate the symbolism of the Old Testament.
It is what takes place in men's spirits which satisfies the
heart of God. The more beautiful and ornate the buildings—the more lavish the pews—the the more pleasing the
music—the more colorful the decorations—the more hindrance there is to pure, spiritual worship. We are in an
era when all the things of God are true and real, and therefore in the spirit.

Worship by the Spirit

This means the energy and power for such can only be by the Spirit of God. We worship by the Spirit of God. Thus we have our Lord speaking of this very thing in John 7:37-38: "In the last day, that great day of the feast, Jesus stood and cried, saying, If any man thirst, let him come unto Me, and drink. He that believeth on Me, as the scripture hath said, out of his belly shall flow rivers of living water."

He follows this with an exposition of His own words: "This spake He of the Spirit, which they that believe on Him should receive: for the Holy Ghost was not yet given; because that Jesus was not yet glorified." Real, inward, spiritual exercise needs the prompting, the presence, and the power of the Holy Spirit. Thus the worship of God in the Spirit and by the Spirit would, in an altogether new way, begin on the day of Pentecost.

We seem to recognize this in the matter of spiritual works—that only the presence and power of the Holy Spirit can seal the Word of God—cause blind eyes to open and frozen feelings to melt—lay pride in the dust—disperse strong prejudice—and open hearts for the Lord to enter. But this is also so in the matter of true worship. Without the Holy Spirit's aid, we cannot worship. Without His energy, our worship will not rise. Without His power, we are flesh-bound.

How different, then, is worship by the Spirit! The Lord said of the life of the indwelling Spirit: "[It] shall be in him a well of water springing up into everlasting life" (John 4:14). The tendency is to bypass this and emphasize the outflow of John 7:38: "Out of his belly shall flow rivers of living water." The emphasis in our day has changed the order of things so that service comes first, and worship is tacked on where a few moments can be found for it. But the springing up of the living water comes before the flowing out. In God's order, worship is first; service follows. Surely, surely, our garners would swell with the plenteous produce of immortal souls if we were first a worshiping people.

For the blessed Holy Spirit,
  Sent by Thee from Heav'n above;
We would join to praise Thee, Father,
  For this matchless Gift of love.

O, forbid that we should grieve Him
  By neglect or willful sin;
Grant that we may know the fullness
  Of this heav'nly Guest within!

For the Holy Spirit's presence,
  Comforter and Guide divine;
From our hearts we join to praise Thee
  For this gracious Gift of Thine.

ALFRED P. GIBBS

THE BURNT OFFERING

It is a burnt sacrifice, an offering made by fire, of a
sweet savour unto the LORD (Leviticus 1:17).

The five offerings in the beginning of the book of Leviticus foreshadow the sacrifice of our Lord on Calvary's cross.
In Exodus we read of God's people groaning under bondage.
In Leviticus, after redemption is effected, they become a
worshiping people. Within a divinely patterned and erected
Tabernacle, they worship in God's appointed way. The golden
key to these offerings is Christ in His grace and work. All the
action honors God, and the burnt offering takes the lead.

The Sacrifice

There were degrees of devotion in what was offered by
the offerer. It could be a male from the herd, a sheep, or even
a small bird. If the offering was from the herd (Leviticus 1:3),

it had to be an unblemished male, which spoke of perfection and strength. It was choice and prime. It represented strength in fullest vigor and beauty unto perfection. That was the highest degree of devotion.

The quality of the offering itself pointed to the suitability of the Lord Jesus as the only acceptable offering to God. He is as strong as God can be—and needed to be so in order to bear the awful burden of human sin. Only He who was girded with omnipotence could carry such a load—for sin was the weightiest of all burdens.

The offerer had to exercise his personal desire to present his offering. There was no compulsion. There was to be no reluctance. It was to be a willing offering. Here we see the free and happy offering of a devoted heart. Such a one knows sin's miserable burden. He also knows the value of redeeming love. There is nothing formal here. There is nothing cold and dead. Faith is a willing grace.

The offerer then put his hand on the offering's head (Leviticus 1:4). This was an act of transference. It was the only way he could be rid of his burden. In figure all his sin was placed on the head of his offering. Nothing was to be retained. The whole sum of his sins was transferred to that which typified the Saviour's head. This, again, was the exercise of faith. There was no way for sin to be dealt with save as it was placed on the head of the offering. This sets forth the Lord Jesus as being alone able to bear our sins.

The Sacrifice Slain

"He shall kill the bullock before the LORD" (Leviticus 1:5). That which would be an offering for sin, and the sinner's surety, cannot be spared. Death alone can pay the debt, satisfy the wrath, bear the guilt, and expiate the sin. Thus we see clearly in this type how Christ must die for our sins so that Satan's accusations may be silenced and conscience may end its strife.

The blood of the sacrifice was then sprinkled "round about upon the altar" (Leviticus 1:5). This was a sprinkling of it over a wide area, and here we learn the wide use of the blood to gain all covenant blessings, and the full reward and fruit of the finished work.

The sacrifice was next flayed (1:6). The skin provided raiment for the offerer, which sets forth Christ, our Lord, as "the Lord our righteousness" through whose sacrifice we are clothed with the best robe Heaven can provide—the pure robe of God's own righteousness given the offerer as a free gift.

The limbs of the sacrifice were all separated and thoroughly washed (1:9). That which stands as a type of Jesus must be perfectly clean. There must be no speck of impurity, for "[God] is of purer eyes than to behold . . . iniquity." All the sacrifice, in all its parts, was then placed on the altar and the fire consumed it all to ashes (1:9). The fire speaks of wrath from God against sin. It is a token of His righteous judgment. Sin cannot be spared, though it is God's beloved Son who bears it. Justice demands that sin be punished—each sin—every sin.

But Jesus bears it all. The agony of His sacrifice is in bearing this wrath of God. Every part of the sacrifice of old was wrapped in awful flame of fire until each part was fully consumed. That is the picture of the awful price paid by our Lord for our redemption; because He has borne it, such fire can never rekindle upon us.

The Sacrifice Sealed

It is "a burnt sacrifice, an offering made by fire, of a sweet savour unto the LORD" (Leviticus 1:9). This is the witness of God's Holy Spirit, written for the everlasting comfort of the redeemed. It is the witness of Heaven, the seal of God, the sweet assurance that the sacrifice of God's beloved Son is fully acceptable to God. It is "a sweet savour." It satisfies every attribute of the divine nature. It provides God ground upon which He can forgive in a righteous way. It gives Him a channel to communicate His peace and joy to the offerer. What wisdom! What love!

We should never come to the Lord's supper without some solemn thought of what is sin's due. What a terrible end it must be to be without Christ, when He, the Son of God, had to suffer so. Who could bear God's awful wrath? That is what hell is! How thankful we should be that the Lord Jesus has borne that for us.

How we should extoll God's wondrous grace! All our sins were laid upon Jesus our Lord, and no more remain to fall upon our heads. What marvelous grace that He, who is the Lord of glory, would condescend to take up our vile sins and bear their awful doom. This is what John Bunyan called "grace abounding to the chief of sinners."

> Lord, e'en to death Thy love could go,
>   A death of shame and loss,
> To vanquish for us every foe,
>   And break the strong man's force.
>
> O, what a load was Thine to bear,
>   Alone in that dark hour,
> Our sins in all their terror there,
>   God's wrath and Satan's pow'r!
>
> The storm that bowed Thy blessed head,
>   Is hushed forever now,
> And rest divine is ours instead,
>   Whilst glory crowns Thy brow.

H. L. ROSSIER
Tr. by MISS C. A. WELLESLEY

THE MEAT OFFERING

> When any will offer a meat offering unto the LORD, his offering shall be of fine flour (Leviticus 2:1).

The varied offerings are to show us different aspects of the Saviour's sacrifice in figure. Each offering is to illustrate the redemption which our Lord purchased for us. These ancient Scriptures are a mine of wealth. They show more of Christ than what most believers ever discern.

The meat offering is the second of the five. God's wisdom has termed it "the meat offering." There are those who try to find strange explanations for the title, since there is none of what we call meat in it. But it is rightly so called, since the term for meat simply means food, and not some kind of flesh. This particular offering was to supply food for the priest.

The Substance of the Offering

The chief material was fine flour (Leviticus 2:1). It is the infinite mind of God which selected the substance, so the thought is deep. And, may we ask, by what process is flour formed? It is formed from earthgrown grain which is threshed from the husk and ground in a mill to a powder. Faith so easily discerns in this the story of our Lord's life on earth. He was born into this arena. No blow was spared Him. He was buffeted with all the fury of men and devils, and even the justice of His own holy law crushed Him.

The flour was fine flour. There were no lumps, no vestiges of unevenness. This sets forth the Saviour's sinless character and the perfect evenness of His temperament. He is the perfect Man and, therefore, the perfect offering.

Oil was added (2:1)—the blessed emblem in Scripture of the Holy Spirit's anointing. The Lord, we read, is given the Spirit "not by measure" (John 3:34). The Holy Spirit formed His body (Luke 1:35), descended upon Him in baptism (Luke 3:22), aided Him in His temptations (Luke 4:1), upheld Him on Calvary's cross (Hebrews 9:14), and aided Him in breaking the bands of death (1 Peter 3:18). The Lord Jesus was rich in the Spirit's anointing.

Frankincense was then sprinkled (Leviticus 2:1). This was to give the offering a sweet fragrance and to fill man's senses with sweet joy. It gave perfume to the people's hearts. It spoke of Him whose name was "as ointment poured forth" (Song of Solomon 1:3).

No leaven and no honey could be brought (Leviticus 2:11). Leaven changes the meal and is an emblem of evil. Leaven spreads its influence throughout, and so is forbidden. Honey is sweet, but ferments, and in this it expresses the tempting power of sin, which at the end proves to be wormwood and gall.

But salt was added (2:13). Salt repels corruption and arrests decay. It brought freshness and taste to the offering, and in this, too, we see blessed features of our Lord. He is all that to the believing offerer. His love is an everlasting covenant of salt.

Thus, in every part of the substance of the meat offering we see Jesus our Lord portrayed in the precious character that He is. There is nothing more gladdening to the soul than the intrinsic perfection of His holy life. The meat offering is a mirror in which we see the absolute perfection of every virtue.

The Use of the Offering

The use is very clearly set forth. In the first place, it satisfied God. We see this, in that part of the offering was to be burned on the altar "to be an offering made by fire, of a sweet savour unto the LORD" (2:2). This part was consumed by fire to show God's wrath against sin which fell upon His beloved Son, and the burning meal sets forth the Lord in His anguish. "O 'tis a wondrous sight!" Thomas Kelly wrote in a hymn. Sin must have torment. It is a high offense to the honor of God. It cannot escape His wrath. So the Lord Jesus must bear it. The fire of vengeance does not spare. God "spared not His own Son." But our Lord so exhausted that wrath that there is none left for His believing people to bear.

Then, a second use of the offering was that it provided food. The remaining part "shall be Aaron's and his sons': it is a thing most holy of the offerings of the LORD made by fire" (2:3). It shows Christ as the Provider for His people—the true Bread of life for hungry souls—the substantial and satisfying food for all who believe. "My flesh is meat indeed, and My blood is drink indeed" (John 6:55).

"Eat, O friends; drink, yea, drink abundantly, O beloved," says Song of Solomon 5:1. And faith brings the hungry to the banqueting table. Faith partakes of Christ and feasts upon Him. There is no other way to gain strength for the journey heavenwards. The soul must feed on Christ if it would endure all the way.

All must offer. As we saw in the burnt offering, so here in the meat offering there are diverse ways of preparing the offering. With some—"baken" in an oven; with others—"baken" in a pan; with still others—"baken" in a frying pan. All such things have infinite and profound meaning. But let it suffice for now that these different utensils, one or another, may be used by all—the rich with their grand ovens down to the poor with their humble hearths. But all must offer. There is no other Christ to offer, whether the offerer be rich or poor. Bring this offering of Christ to God and, no matter what your station in life, you will be accepted of Him, and you will be fully fed and satisfied.

> What food luxurious loads the board
> When, at His table, sits the Lord!
> The wine how rich, the bread how sweet,
> When Jesus deigns His guests to meet!
>
> If now, with eyes defiled and dim,
> We see the signs, but see not Him;
> O, may His love the scales displace,
> And bid us see Him face to face!
>
> Thou glorious Bridegroom of our hearts,
> Thy present smile a heav'n imparts!
> O, lift the veil, if veil there be,
> Let ev'ry saint Thy glory see!
>
> CHARLES H. SPURGEON

THE PEACE OFFERING

A sacrifice of peace offering (Leviticus 3:1).

Peace is what mankind has ever sought; but peace lives, and can be found, only in the Lord Jesus Christ. Peace was announced by His coming. Declared the angels at His birth, "On earth peace." Sin brought in enmity, but the scheme by which peace could be replanted in the heart of man was modeled in the ancient peace offering.

The Mark of the Offering

The offering could be a male or female and taken from cattle, sheep, or goats (Leviticus 3:1,6,12). This made the offering possible to all classes and so readily at hand. No man would have to search very far for such an offering. And so readily obtainable is our blessed Saviour—always at hand. He is never beyond the reach of any.

The offering, since it was a model of Christ, was to be free from fault. Any fault would have debarred Christ our Lord from being an acceptable offering to a holy God. Only a sinless offering could make a sufficient sacrifice for sins for others. Had there been sin in the Lord Jesus Himself, then He would have been forced to make sacrifice for Himself.

The offerer then placed his hands on his offering and thus portrayed the transfer of guilt. Thus the burden of it no longer rested upon the offerer but upon the offering.

The appointed offering was then slain (3:2). Death is the God-appointed desert of sin, but now through grace we see how it falls on Christ our Lord, as here in the model. This was the price of peace—the only means by which peace could be purchased.

The Division of the Offering

The offering was divided into three parts. First, there was a part for God. This was the best and choicest. It was placed on the altar and was consumed by fire (3:3-5). Thus the first part is brought to God, and in the fire's consuming of it we see again the wrath of God against the sin of man. Justice in God demands this display of wrath, or else God's holy character would be forfeited. The honor of His character could only be maintained by the God-Man slain. Only the Lord Jesus could meet the demand of God's justice and man's sins.

Secondly, provision is made for those who minister and serve. The Lord is never debtor to any man; they who leave all for Him in order to do Him service, have the needs of their own souls fully met. Their food is the same as that which satisfies God. Let all who serve as ministering brethren, or missionaries at home or abroad, or elders or deacons in the local church, know that their spiritual strength for service is through Christ as their peace offering. They cannot labor unless they feed on the Lord. This alone can produce the energy which will never flag, and gird the loins with sufficient strength for every demanding duty.

Thirdly, the offerer takes his portion. The essence of true faith lies in the partaking of our Lord—the inward receiving of Him. It is not mental knowledge—light in the head, the outward handling of truth—which brings peace. It is feeding by faith upon Christ as our offering of peace.

Here warning is given by the Lord that the unclean may not partake (Leviticus 7:20). Impurity will never lead to peace with God, most holy. God has provided means for the cleansing away of all sin, but neglect of such means cannot bring about such a gracious end. They who sit down without a wedding garment are cast out (Matthew 22:13). "There is no peace, saith the LORD, unto the wicked" (Isaiah 48:22).

The Motive of the Offerer

The offerer was first prompted by a sense of gratitude. His debts had been large, but now have been paid. His substitute has paid to the full. This then prompted another exercise— the offerer vowed and made pledge to live for God (Leviticus 7:12,16). These two resolutions were fair flowers which now began to bloom in the life of the offerer after peace had been made.

The heart of those who have experienced such peace should ever be full, and ever flowing forth in ceaseless praise. Who could count the number of God's mercies? Who could withhold his songs of praise? But should not gratitude lead to dedication, and to a purposeful resolve of heart to devote one's life to the service of such a Saviour?

But none can praise, and none can serve, until peace is made with God. Such praise can rise, and such service can be given, only where peace abounds. These great exercises of the soul were to be done without delay. "It shall be eaten the same day that he offereth his sacrifice." No remnant left to the third day was to be touched (7:17). There was to be no delay, no vacillation, no lingering, no reluctance. So with us today. The Lord Jesus has spread the feast. He bids us sit down with instant joy. It is ours to partake without a moment's hesitation. The feast is set "to guide our feet into the way of peace."

> Oh, the peace forever flowing
>   From God's thoughts of His own Son!
> Oh, the peace of simply knowing
>   On the cross that all was done.
>
> Peace with God! the blood in Heaven
>   Speaks of pardon now to me:
> Peace with God! the Lord is risen!
>   Righteousness now counts me free.

Peace with God is Christ in glory;
God is just and God is love;
Jesus died to tell the story,
Foes to bring to God above.

A. P. CECIL

THE SIN OFFERING

Let him bring for his sin, which he hath sinned, a young bullock without blemish unto the LORD for a sin offering (Leviticus 4:3).

Sin is a word with an ominous sound. The word is one of the briefest, but the thing itself dragged angels down from Heaven and ruined our God-created humanity. Our Lord's cross flung a new and divine light upon sin as the abominable thing which God hates. There was sin upon the earth before the Christ of God died, but it was imperfectly known.

Sin is no trifle with God—it is something He could not overlook. It is something at which God pointed His finger and said in effect, "I hate that, and that, and that." It marred the beauty of His creation. It brought forth weeds and thorns, and spawned natural calamity. It wrecked a beauteous world.

Sin was man's ruin. It drove man out of peaceful fellowship with God. It made him a hardened rebel. It brought his mind into total spiritual darkness, his affections into a nest of unclean birds, his will into a den of God-defying schemes. Worst of all, it was the mother of death. It has dug every grave since the world began, and filled the homes of earth's inhabitants with grief and sorrow. But it reaches beyond death, and has built the prison house of hell, where all is eternal woe. God's curse is upon it.

The sin offering of Israel is designed to teach us the horrors of sin, and the terrible cost of expiation, but to display, also, the wonders of redeeming grace. The ancient rite in Israel's law shows the way of escape. The dire consequences of sin need not fall upon the sinner's head. There is a way of escape from the dread penalty. Its stain can be cleansed away. The debt may be forgiven.

The Good Tidings

Justice and holiness in God demand that each sin bear a merited punishment. Each violation of law must drink the condemnation. With such strong demands from law, the Son of God comes forth from Heaven to save us by meeting the stern terms. He takes the place of the guilty. He stands forth as the representative of His people. He assumes responsibility for all their sins. He suffers for each and all of their sins. Only because He is God can He absorb so much punishment.

But He is the complete sin offering. He pays with His own precious blood. He endures the full and awful wrath of God against the sin of man. His manhood qualifies Him to do this, and His deity upholds Him. It is thus that sin is fully punished, and the redeemed are fully saved. All who believe live and walk in freedom from sin.

The Offender and His Sacrifice

There are differences in men. The first offender here is the priest himself—to teach us that the very holiest of men are sinners, and that none can approach God without an adequate sin offering. Sin has allured, and snared, and defiled the best of men. Even the priest in Israel's ancient ceremonials must see his own guilt and his need for pardon. Thus he must bring an unblemished young bullock to the tabernacle door. This is a God-given direction, and the offering is a God-chosen one. God Himself has decreed the plan of redemption. He willed the ransom, and His Son achieved it through the Spirit's aid. The sin offering of Israel speaks of the Saviour to come and clearly shows how atonement is provided by Him.

The offender's hands must be placed on the victim's head. This is the transmission of his guilt. The sin of the offender thus passes to the sin offering. Here we are instructed how to roll our sins upon Christ as our Sin-Bearer. And the wages of sin is death. The soul that sinneth must die. Sin and its fruits and penalties are absolute certainties. Whoever bears sin must hear judicial doom before the righteous Judge. If God's beloved Son bear our sins, then there can be for Him no mitigation of the punishment. God cannot lower His demands, nor abate any of His wrath against sin, even in the case of His beloved Son acting as Substitute.

The Uses of the Blood

The first use of blood is that the veil is sprinkled seven times (Leviticus 4:6). The veil hung before the mercy seat and was the entrance into the holiest of all. This sprinkling means that those who would pass into God's immediate presence—into His holy Heaven—must be blood-sprinkled. There can be no coming to God without sin-removing blood.

Secondly, the blood was put on the horns of the golden altar (4:7). This was the place from which sweet incense rose, emblem of ascending prayer. Our Lord's intercession for us prevails because of His shed blood. The blood of Jesus is our strength in its supplication. Nothing can ascend to God, most holy, until it is washed clean from all pollutants. What we are and have must be washed by His blood.

Thirdly, the remainder of the blood was poured out at the bottom of the brazen altar (4:7). Thus all is used to bring assurance to the heart. Each drop of blood has its value. Our atonement needs the whole of our Lord's sacrifice—all His blood—and the whole is freely given.

The Shame Heaped on the Offering

When the costliest parts were burnt on the altar, we see more than substitutionary death. The sin offering had to be an accursed thing. So then, the remnant of the victim was borne outside the camp and was consumed with fire. This is a picture of Christ made a curse for us (Galatians 3:13; Hebrews 13:11). He is cast out as earth's refuse. The curse falls upon the Saviour's cross—"made a curse"—how awful! What a price for Him to pay!

> Alas! and did my Saviour bleed?
> And did my Sovereign die?
> Would He devote that sacred head
> For such a worm as I?
>
> Was it for crimes that I have done
> He groaned upon the tree?
> Amazing pity! grace unknown!
> And love beyond degree!
>
> Thus might I hide my blushing face,
> While His dear cross appears;
> Dissolve my heart in thankfulness,
> And melt my eyes to tears.
>
>   ISAAC WATTS

THE TRESPASS OFFERING

If a soul commit a trespass, and sin through ignorance, in the holy things of the LORD; then he shall bring for his trespass unto the LORD a ram without blemish out of the flocks, with thy estimation by shekels of silver, after the shekel of the sanctuary, for a trespass offering. And he shall make amends for the harm that he hath done in the holy thing, and shall add the fifth part thereto, and give it unto the priest: and the priest shall make an atonement for him

with the ram of the trespass offering, and it shall be forgiven
him (Leviticus 5:15-16).

Sin has many forms, and everything it touches it wounds
and imparts death. These verses state the first case of the trespass offering. It is the case of a soul sinning through ignorance.
God's law has been infringed, and His holy will set at nought.
But, though done in ignorance, it is no trifle with God. That,
sin can never be. Every form of iniquity is hated by God.
God's white throne would lose its pristine whiteness if any sin
were condoned.

The Offense

This rite especially condemns transgression in holy things.
What would such transgression be? It could be trying to
be righteous by one's own merits. It is Cain religion—bringing to God the fruit of one's own toil—choosing the rags of
our own righteousness, rather than the gospel robe of God's
free gift of righteousness. This trespass has a fair exterior, but
it slays the soul.

There is much of it in our world. All human religions invented by man are typical of sins of trespass in holy things—
religions such as Hinduism, Mohammedanism, Buddhism,
Confucianism, and all cults which deny the Godhood of the
Lord Jesus and His finished atoning work on Calvary's cross.
Devotees of such will not take up God's plan, and they refuse
to be taught the way of God. They invent their own way.

But, again, the trespass can be seen in those who know
the truth of God, but bring to Him no more than the ceremonial round, the regular attendance, a fair contribution of
money, the faithful adherence to the church creed—all such
as if sufficient to secure the crown of life. So many believe—
alas, to their ruin.

Both these ways lead to woe. They are simply opposing
falsehoods. Both are Satan's delusion. Such trespasses live only
in dens of ignorance. But though spawned in ignorance, they
are still trespasses.

The Substitute

Once again we see the dying victim as the picture-type proclaiming Christ the Lord. He is the trespass offering. He is "made . . . sin for us." He suffers all our deserved punishment. He drinks up all our woe.

This is the amazing grace which is the eternal song of the saved. This is the "joy unspeakable and full of glory." This is the hope set before us, which is as an anchor of the soul, sure and steadfast. The trespass offering bleeds and dies, and only by such substitution can the offender be forgiven. So Jesus dies, and all His family of believing people are saved. And "Who shall lay any thing to the charge of God's elect? It is God that justifieth. Who is he that condemneth? It is Christ that died" (Romans 8:33-34).

The Repayment

The need of sinful man is vast. None can measure the dimensions of guilt's trespass, but the work of our Lord covers it all. Here we see that the value of the trespass must be reckoned. The cost must be paid according to the sanctuary's weight—not what man feels is the value. Thus here in this ancient rite we see a fifth part added. It is not enough to give equal. There must be excess (Leviticus 5:16).

Why is this? Because trespass defrauds God. Sin is not only an offense against a law but a defrauding of God. Nothing we have or are is our own. Everything, therefore, which God has given us should be used to do Him honor and augment His praise. But we have robbed God of this! It would be vain conceit, too, to imagine we ourselves could make it up to Him. The debt is huge, and only God's beloved Son can pay it. No devotedness can repay. Surplus of merit is but a papist's dream. All our works only increase our debt, only deepen bankruptcy.

Thus the trespass offerer added a surplus. Who can measure the surplus which the Lord Jesus Christ brought to Cal-

vary's cross? In that cross is all that God can give and all that
God can take. This makes the offering of Christ so full and
rich, so precious and divine. Let us acknowledge before God
that trespass stains our hearts, that we do often trespass
even in holy things.

Let us remember that this form of trespass is as offensive
to God as vulgar sin. It raises the same barrier between the
soul and God. But here in the trespass offering the Lord Jesus
is depicted again in the brightest hues. He died to pay the
trespass offering. Only as we cling to Him can our trespass be
forgiven. His cross is the only expiation for every trespass, as
well as for every sin. His cross is a sufficient expiation. His
surplus payment is more than enough.

> Worthy of homage and of praise;
>   Worthy by all to be adored:
> Exhaustless theme of heavenly lays!
>   Thou, Thou art worthy, Jesus, Lord.
>
> To Thee, e'en now, our song we raise,
>   Tho' sure the tribute mean must prove:
> No mortal tongue can tell Thy ways,
>   So full of light and life and love.
>
> Yet, Saviour, Thou shalt have full praise:
>   We soon shall meet Thee in the cloud,
> We soon shall see Thee face to face,
>   In glory praising as we would.

MISS F. T. WIGRAM

11

THE SANCTITY OF BLOOD

Whatsoever man there be of the house of Israel, or of
the strangers that sojourn among you, that eateth any manner of blood; I will even set My face against that soul that
eateth blood, and will cut him off from among his people.

> For the life of the flesh is in the blood: and I have given it
> to you upon the altar to make an atonement for your souls
> (Leviticus 17:10-11).

This ordinance warns that no common use may be made
of blood. It is fenced around most rigidly with the sternest of
divine decrees. None must eat it. No lips must taste it.

The Type

Blood is set apart. Since God has designed it to be so,
there must be a high and holy purpose for this. It is sanctified because it points to Calvary's cross. It shadows forth the
death of God's beloved Son and the price of our redemption.
It stood forth in those ancient days as a picture of the very
life of God's Lamb of atonement. Its shedding is the symbol
of death.

After the flood of Noah's day, God enlarged man's diet,
and no longer was man to live without flesh to eat. Even so,
there was this solemn prohibition: "Flesh with the life thereof, which is the blood thereof, shall ye not eat" (Genesis 9:4).

So all through the ages until our Lord came, Heaven's
authoritative voice banned the partaking of blood in the diet.
It was devoted to God. It was most holy unto Him. It set forth
in figurative form the suffering and death of the Redeemer as
He would make atonement for our souls. There was a holiness
about blood which demanded reverence from men. None were
permitted to forget the sacrifice which God purported to
make in the fullness of time.

The Antitype

We live in a different dispensation than that of the Old
Testament. That wondrous death of God's Beloved is no more
veiled in types and figures. The cross of Christ has been raised.
He has hung there, and died there, and His side has been
opened to release that which alone can cleanse from sin and
wash away every stain.

The antitype of the blood shed on Jewish altars is the precious blood of Christ. That blood is unique and precious because of Him whose blood it is. It would not seem that He who hung on Calvary's cross had blood different from that of any other man. The natural eye could not perceive that! Man, Jesus was, but not man of Adam's race. Blood He had, but not the polluted blood of fallen man.

He who hung on Calvary's cross was not man only, but the mighty God. Deity was enshrined in the body that hung on that cross, in that body which had been mauled and disfigured by wicked men. Godhood He has, and Godhood is His right. It is not a man only who suffered on the cross; it is God. The life of the flesh is in the blood. Blood is the symbol of life—therefore our Lord's blood is essentially the life of God (Acts 20:28).

There is a preciousness, then, in such blood which could not be accumulated by all the blood of all sinless beings if blood they had. Myriads of angels could never die the death the Lord Jesus died, nor could their pains suffice to pay the debt of human sin. Jesus is God, and therefore brings a life symbolized in His blood, which is essentially divine. Therefore it is sufficient as a sacrifice and must by its nature meet every demand.

The Efficacy

Its efficacy no tongue can tell. It will be the incessant praise of the redeemed throughout the countless ages of eternity. It is the ransom price of all the saved ones—and the number of them is countless. Nothing but the blood of Jesus has saved them. No claim of law can be made against them. No chain can bind them. No adversary can accuse them. At one time the woes of sin, the terrors of the law, and the accusing finger of conscience denounced them. It seemed as though Heaven was frowning upon them, and hell was waiting to receive them.

But now all this alarm is past. A new day has dawned, and it sprang forth from the cross of our Lord Jesus Christ.

The Word of God came with divine authority: "Though your sins be as scarlet, they shall be as white as snow; though they be red like crimson, they shall be as wool" (Isaiah 1:18). Faith believes it, and finds it is so.

How we should meditate on the blood! When we wake in the morning, go through the day, and come to rest at night, this should be ever in our thought. Angels desire to look into the mystery and power of it, but can do no more than wonder and adore. For us who believe, it is salvation's door, the way to Heaven.

How we should love the precious blood! It is the proof that God loves us and that the beloved Son of God loves us better than Himself. Prize His blood. Let it sit high on the throne of our affections. Let us hold it in fond embrace and never let it go.

How we should use His blood! It needs to be used every hour—all the time. Use it in the battle with Satan. Use it in prayer. Use it in service. Use it in life, and use it in death. It is precious in God's sight. Let it forever be precious in ours.

> Not all the blood of beasts,
>   On Jewish altars slain,
> Could give the guilty conscience peace,
>   Or wash away its stain.
>
> But Christ, the heavenly Lamb,
>   Took all our sins away,
> A sacrifice of nobler name
>   And richer blood than they.
>
> We now look back to see
>   The burden Thou didst bear,
> When hanging on the accursed tree,
>   For all our guilt was there.

ISAAC WATTS

12

THE SCAPEGOAT

> And Aaron shall cast lots upon the two goats; one lot
> for the LORD, and the other lot for the scapegoat (Leviticus
> 16:8).

There is great power in words. There may be even more
power in pictures. Pictures seem to live and register in our
minds better than words. So God has given us a world of
moving models in the Old Testament, and these proclaim in
detail His profoundest truths. They are models which point
to Christ, and the Spirit of God has made them suitable to
every grade of student, so that even the smallest child can
understand them. One of the most living of these models is
Israel's great day of atonement.

On this day many animal victims died. The stream of
blood was deep and wide. This abundant death proclaimed
the awful curse of sin. But each sacrifice also proclaimed God's
remedy for sin, and sounded out the truth of redemption.
These sacrifices, then, were heralds of Christ. On the day of
atonement two goats were brought for a sin offering. The high
priest received them at the door of the Tabernacle and cast lots.

The casting of the lot meant that the selection was left
to God. Of these two goats, one was selected for death, the
other to live as the scapegoat. In this selection of the two
goats we see a picture of God selecting His beloved Son in
the councils of eternal love. The beloved Son was called to
execute the saving work because He alone was adequate.

The First Goat

The first goat had to die. Its blood was shed. With this
blood the high priest then entered into the holy of holies.

46

There he sprinkled it on the mercy seat, and seven times on the horns of the altar, and on the tent of meeting. This extensive use of the blood was to show the extensiveness of sin. It is a widespread malady. It is found everywhere man moves. But the blood shed is also man's purchase price. It meets every demand of justice. It pays all dues to law. It settles all debts. The blood of Christ thus sprinkles every page of a believer's life, and blots out all his sins.

The same blood is our peace. When conscience is awakened by the Spirit of God, it writhes in agony. It is sore wounded at the remembrance of sins, and can find no rest. It cries, as David did, "Against Thee, Thee only, have I sinned, and done this evil in Thy sight" (Psalm 51:4). Such an awakened heart finds no rest, no forgiveness, and no deliverance until it comes to the mercy seat and to the blood of sprinkling. That blood has fourfold power.

(1) *Sin-destroying power.* Sin is like a weed with many roots. The sins of men have spread far and wide and they rise up in every season. Nothing can destroy these vile weeds but the touch of the Saviour's blood. Let poor souls look to the Saviour's cross and see what the blessed Son of God did to sin. He destroyed it completely.

(2) *Satan-defeating power.* There is no place on earth which does not bear traces of Satan's presence or influence. No palace of kings, no shacks of the poor have ever shut him out. He has the key to every home and to every room in the home. Nothing can defeat his evil designs and overcome that evil influence but the precious blood of Christ the Lord. Satan flees before the ensign of the cross.

(3) *Hell-defying power.* Hell cannot receive a blood-washed soul. Its chains cannot bind such a one. Its fires cannot burn him. The gnawing worm cannot torment him. The blood of Jesus is the only safeguard against the pains of hell.

(4) *Heaven-delivering power.* The blood of Christ removes every hindrance in the way to Heaven. When you look into Heaven and see the great throng and you ask: "What are these?"—the answer is: "They which . . . have washed their robes, and made them white in the blood of the Lamb" (Rev-

elation 7:13,14). No other cleansing can avail to make sinners fit for such a holy place as God's Heaven.

The Second Goat

Now the second goat appears. This is the scapegoat. The high priest stretches out his hands and lays them on its head. It is a token of transmitted guilt. The high priest confesses all the sins of his people—a fearful catalog. The scapegoat receives the burden. It takes the load off the people of God.

The scapegoat is then led away. Those transmitted sins are borne beyond the camp, beyond where man can ever discover them, beyond the far borders of a waste wilderness. The goat disappears into the thickets of an untrodden waste, never to be found again.

This is to show what God has done with the sins of His people. All our sins were laid upon Jesus. "The LORD hath laid on Him the iniquity of us all" (Isaiah 53:6). And listen to what He has done with them: "As far as the east is from the west, so far hath He removed our transgressions from us" (Psalm 103:12). None can measure that distance. It is an infinite separation. "Thou wilt cast all their sins into the depths of the sea" (Micah 7:19). No line can reach them. They are sunk in immeasurable depths. They are forever hid in a very deep grave.

"Thou hast cast all my sins behind Thy back" (Isaiah 38:17). Eyes with forward bent cannot see them. They are hid in the distant rear. "I have blotted out, as a thick cloud, thy transgressions, and, as a cloud, thy sins" (Isaiah 44:22). The blackening clouds, all full of storm and tempest, are not removed only, so that they can blow back another day—but are blotted out to exist no more. They have vanished away.

"They shall not be found," says the Lord in Jeremiah 50:20. The scapegoat confirms this truth, and there is no deeper comfort than to know that all our sins—so many, so vile, so hateful—have been thus removed. The Lord Jesus has taken them away, and God sees His believing people only in the glories of His beloved Son.

O Christ, Thy precious blood was shed,
  For guilty sinners Thou didst die:
My sins were all upon Thee laid,
  On Thee my soul doth now rely.
Thee, Lamb of God, by faith I see,
A perfect Sacrifice for me.

'Twas grace abounding brought Thee down
  From yonder realms of light above;
The cross was Thine, and Thine the crown
  Shall ever be, O Lord of love!
Thy mighty triumph o'er the grave
Declares Thy right the lost to save.

Author Unknown

13

THE DRINK OFFERING

The drink offering thereof shall be of wine (Leviticus 23:13).

Wine, which cheereth God and man (Judges 9:13).

On most occasions in the tabernacle ceremonies of the Old Testament, wine was outpoured and, as a drink offering, completed the worship. A cup was there and, in the cup, a wine offering. The revealing rays of the Spirit make faith to fly from this to the last paschal feast which our Lord interrupted to inaugurate His own remembrance feast. It was here that our Lord took a cup full of the juice of the vine, uplifted His thanks, then gave the cup to His little flock, saying, "This is My blood of the new testament, which is shed for many for the remission of sins" (Matthew 26:28).

Thus wine is a gospel sign. It takes its place among the holiest of symbols. "This is My blood!" And this symbol is the key which opens to us the treasure of the drink offering of old. It is one of the choicest emblems of redeeming grace.

The blood which streamed from Calvary's cross is of infinite and exceeding preciousness. It speaks first of our Lord's true manhood. Jesus had blood, or else He could not have been man. Without blood, He could not have been a true kinsman of our race. And He must be true man if He would be man's Surety. He must have blood to be truly man.

But let us never forget that He assumes this manhood without ceasing to be God. His blood, symbol of life, is man's blood, yet divine. The blood is God's, yet human. This is a most profound mystery to us mortal men, and we can never fathom the uniqueness of the Person of the Lord Jesus Christ.

We now go forward to Calvary's cross to see our Lord pouring forth His blood. Until this precious blood flows, there is no remission of sin (Hebrews 9:22). But our Lord does not withhold His blood. It begins to fall in circumcision when He is eight days old, later in Gethsemane's garden, then when scourged, again when He is crowned with thorns; finally, it is fully outpoured at the cross. His brow, His hands, His feet, His side, His heart—all weep blood. This is the sure proof that atonement has been made! Without the shedding of blood no sin could be forgiven—no atonement made. But in the shedding of His most precious blood, our Lord paid a full redemption price for us, and made salvation possible to all men everywhere.

In Scripture wine also speaks of joy. "Wine, which cheereth God and man." Thus blood and joy are joined together. And that joy is marvelous.

Joy To God

From all eternity God has willed to have a human race of exultant souls with Him in Heaven. That was ever the divine intention. But a mighty barrier interposed. Sin came between God and man and separated them. How, then, can this barrier be removed? Sin has dug a very deep abyss for man. How can sin-fettered souls and sin-defiled man enter God's holy Heaven? Jesus came and took away the barrier, and God now sees believers complete in Him. The great sacrifice on the cross cleared the way for God by grace to execute and fulfill His plans.

Joy To Angels

Angels, too, yearned that fallen man be saved. When a sinful man becomes saved, we read that there is a mighty outburst of celestial joy among the angels of Heaven (Luke 15:10). If this is so over one sinner that repenteth, what loud praises there must be over the whole multitude of the redeemed! All this happy rejoicing among the angels of Heaven is made possible through the sacrificial death of the Lord Jesus. The angels of Heaven know well that if all of them together had consented to die, such corporate death could not have saved a single sinner. They know who He was who died on Calvary's cross, and thus they cry: "Worthy is the Lamb that was slain." He is the supreme delight of the angels.

Joy To Men

Peter speaks of this joy to men as "unspeakable" (1 Peter 1:8)—that is, something beyond adequate expression. Gratitude can only utter its thanks in feeble praise and joyful song. Through the outpouring of this precious blood by the Son of God, the great Creator God (the sovereign Ruler over all things) becomes the portion of believers. He becomes their Father and their God, and they have access to His smile and favor. The heart of man can know no happier throb than to be able to look up into the face of the living God, the blessed and only Potentate, and say, "My Father!"

Men search for happiness in vain if they seek it not in Christ the Lord. God can never give joy to any man apart from faith in His beloved Son—for there is no other channel of conveyance for that joy save through His Son and the sacrifice He made for sin. The blood of the Lord Jesus, in symbol, is in this cup. Here, in the wine which the cup contains, is the emblem of His most precious blood, and in the pouring out of that blood you can read all the heart of God—and the travail and passion of His great love for us. Let our souls rise in heavenly joy and grateful praise unto Him who loved us, and gave Himself for us. May we adore Him forever!

> Rejoice and be glad!
>   The Redeemer has come!
> Go look on His cradle,
>   His cross and His tomb.
>
>   Chorus:
>   Sound His praises!
>   Tell the story
>   Of Him who was slain!
>   Sound His praises!
>   Tell with gladness
>   He liveth again!
>
> Rejoice and be glad!
>   Now the pardon is free!
> The Just for the unjust
>   Has died on the tree.
>
> Rejoice and be glad!
>   For the Lamb that was slain
> O'er death is triumphant,
>   And liveth again.

HORATIUS BONAR

14

GOD'S BANQUET

He shall eat the bread of his God, both of the most holy, and of the holy (Leviticus 21:22).

These words most probably refer to the shewbread which, interpreted, means "the bread of the presence." It was the bread on the table within the Tabernacle, and associated with Him whose presence was vouchsafed to God's people in all their journeyings. It was different from the manna which fell in the wilderness and which came down from heaven. This was "presence bread," and it was taken from the Lord's table within the sanctuary and given to those who ministered as priests before the Lord.

But since it was made of common wheat, the fruit of the earth, and was ground in the mill, mixed with water, and baked by fire on the hearth, it sets forth some of the glorious charms of the Saviour. It sounds forth the truth of the gospel.

The Provision

In the day when God created man, He graciously made full provision for man's physical needs by providing Eden's garden or fruit-bearing trees. There was rich abundance for Adam and Eve at every turn. Everything was full and ripe in the day of their creation, so that they were well provided for. This is true also of the Lord's new creation, the redeemed of the Lord. He Himself is a garden of good things—for all and every need.

The Lord appeared in flesh here on earth as part of our humanity, but separated from the sinful mass by God's own hand and the Holy Spirit's activity. He was subjected to human conditions—the persecution of men, the fire of God's wrath against sin—till, being "made perfect through sufferings," He became "the bread of God." Israel's bread was not eaten unkneaded, or unbaked, so neither could our Lord become living bread without similar processes of preparation in the Spirit.

He is God's own provision—prepared by God Himself, and freely given to meet our deepest need. "My Father giveth you the true bread from heaven" (John 6:32). There is no buying on our part; no selling on His. All is free. All is the gift of divine love. All in Christ is "the finest of the wheat" for His people. "The bread of the presence" proclaims God's full provision, which is laid up in Jesus for His waiting people. They are indeed loved, cared for, enriched, and strengthened by feasting upon Him. Here in Christ sufficiency abounds while time shall be and when time shall be no more—sufficiency for every need which has been, or shall be, or can be.

Our hunger is deep—our strength a quivering reed—our peril desperate—but the Lord Jesus changes all our empty living into feasts of most suitable and delectable supply. No wonder the prophet cries, "Wherefore do ye spend money for that which is not bread? and your labour for that which satisfieth not? hearken diligently unto Me, and eat ye that which is good, and let your soul delight itself in fatness" (Isaiah 55:2).

The Participants

The provision was for the priests—God's priesthood. Before them, however, God Himself was a partaker of His own spread feast. That which is for the satisfaction of His people is also for God's own satisfaction. This is the case in some of the offerings in the early chapters of Leviticus. God takes His share and is satisfied. Every attribute of His divine nature is satisfied in the offering of His beloved Son. It is "a sweet savour unto the LORD." It cheereth God as well as man (Judges 9:13). God's delight was not in the symbols as such, but in all that these represented and embodied—all that was ultimately unfolded in His beloved Son, the Lord Jesus Christ.

It was for His people who, in this age of grace, are all made priests to offer spiritual sacrifices unto God. Surely what satisfies God the Father ought well to delight and satisfy His people! Our Lord is not as the symbol—as Israel's perishing shewbread, often removed and renewed—but He abides the same forever. Each of Israel's feasts and offerings set forth in figure one aspective portrayal of our Lord's fullness.

However, all of these together are but a very scant reflection of what He really is. He is God's fullness, God's feast of fat things, and He is that for His people throughout the countless ages of eternity. What satisfies the believer is that in which God delights. The Lord and His sacrifice regale

Heaven. The Lord and His sacrifice regale earth. The life, the health, the vigor of spiritual life derive from this substantial feast. To feed on Christ refreshes the heart, girds the loins with strength, and brings an energy which can never flag.

Israel's bread was called "the shewbread," or "the presence bread," because it was eaten before the Lord and in the holy place. It was for the priests only; no others could participate. Thus we see that Christ as the Bread of life is only for His redeemed people and is "continual bread"—another interpretation of it. In ancient Israel there always had to be bread on the tabernacle table in order to give the notion, in type, of that which is everlasting in Christ, the true Bread. God feeds upon Him and is satisfied! We feed upon Him and are satisfied! Both God and man sit at the same table and partake of the same bread, even His beloved Son. Thus God and man meet in Christ and have their joint fellowship and joy in Him.

> Here at Thy table, Lord, we meet,
>   To feed on food divine;
> Thy body is the bread we eat,
>   Thy precious blood the wine.
>
> Here praise and pardon sweetly flow;
>   O what delightful food!
> We eat the bread and drink the wine,
>   But think on nobler good.
>
> Sure, there was never love so free,
>   Dear Saviour—so divine;
> Well Thou mayst claim that heart of me,
>   Which owes so much to Thine.
>
> G. FRANC

15

THE LORD'S SUFFERINGS PREDICTED

All things must be fulfilled, which were written in the law of Moses, and in the prophets, and in the psalms, concerning Me (Luke 24:44).

Since the sacrifice of God's beloved Son was settled in the councils of the Godhead before the world began, the Old Testament is full of predictions of it. In the above words, the risen Lord is simply confirming His own teaching during His earthly ministry. Nothing which the Lord ever said had to be corrected or modified or changed. But He did have to open the minds of His disciples to understand Old Testament prediction (Luke 24:45).

The sufferings and death of the Lord Jesus should not have taken the disciples by surprise since they were somewhat familiar with Old Testament Scriptures. Indeed, they should have expected His passion. The pages of the Old Testament sparkle with the jewels of predicted redemption. They stand as a rich tree laden with the promises of God regarding it. We can stand there as on a God-given height of revelation, and from it view all that our Lord was to suffer.

The Lord Jesus is the theme of all Scripture. He is the light and luster of every page. To read the Old Testament aright is a sunlight walk with Him. To read it aright surely opens redemption's plan. But the Jews did not read the Old Testament rightly. They read of His coming kingdom and glory, and understood that! They understood, for instance, Daniel 7:14: "And there was given Him dominion, and glory, and a kingdom, that all people, nations, and languages, should serve Him: His dominion is an everlasting dominion, which shall not pass away, and His kingdom that which shall not be destroyed."

They expected that! But they were blind to the Lord's humiliation, as in Isaiah 53:5, "But He was wounded for our transgressions, He was bruised for our iniquities: the chastisement of our peace was upon Him; and with His stripes we are healed." They could not see that!

After His resurrection the Lord stressed this point: "All things must be fulfilled." There was a Saviour to be given; thus a Saviour to be born; a Saviour who would make adequate sacrifice for sins, the only sacrifice that God would ever accept and call men to bring; a sacrifice that God would never refuse. Thus the sufferings and death of the Lord Jesus are never spoken of in Scripture as a tragic mistake or an unforeseen accident. It was all God's own wise plan to rescue man from Satan's power, and it is all so clearly spelled out in Old Testament Scriptures.

True, there was man's side to the cross. Psalm 22 tells us that He would be compassed about with "bulls"—the Jewish rulers; "dogs"—the Gentile forces of Rome; "lions"—the ferocious hosts of hell. There, too, is depicted man's ribald mockery, derisive laughter, universal scorn. But behind all this there is "the determinate counsel and foreknowledge of God" (Acts 2:23). The crucifying of Christ expresses all the inherent hatred in man's heart against God. But the purposeful laying down of His life was the manifestation of God's utter and complete love for fallen man. There was a divine necessity for the cross; God had no other way of dealing with human sin. It was clear from the beginning.

Old Testament Predictions Spoken by Our Lord

When at Caesarea, our Lord said that "He must go unto Jerusalem, and suffer many things of the elders and chief priests and scribes, and be killed" (Matthew 16:21). Then, in Mark 9:12, He said, "It is written of the Son of man, that He must suffer many things, and be set at nought." Again, in Luke 18:31, "Behold, we go up to Jerusalem, and all things that are written by the prophets concerning the Son of man shall be accomplished."

Also, when Peter tried to stand in the way for our Lord's defense in the garden of Gethsemane, Jesus rebuked him with the words: "Put up . . . thy sword into his place. . . . How then shall the scriptures be fulfilled, that thus it must be?" (Matthew 26:52,54) In His walk to Emmaus with the two journeying there in postresurrection days, the Lord Jesus said, "O fools, and slow of heart to believe all that the prophets have spoken: Ought not Christ to have suffered these things, and to enter into His glory?" (Luke 24:25-26)

Thus the Saviour's sacrifice was written in letters of gold in the Old Testament. God's redemption plan shines forth telling the story that God's beloved Son would come and bear the sinner's sins. All such Scriptures spring from the eternal Spirit of God, and display the sacrifice of God the Son in skillfully constructed symbols and forms.

Old Testament Predictions by the Apostles

Look at Peter's declaration in Acts 3:18, "But those things, which God before had shewed by the mouth of all His prophets, that Christ should suffer, He hath so fulfilled." When Paul is chosen and appointed, there is this remarkable statement by him in Acts 13:27, "For they that dwell at Jerusalem, and their rulers, because they knew Him not, nor yet the voices of the prophets which are read every sabbath day, they have fulfilled them in condemning Him."

Do we fully understand what that means? It means that the Old Testament Scriptures were read in Jewish synagogues every sabbath through centuries of time. The prophets cried of a death which would save from death, of a stream of blood which would cleanse away all sin, of a Messiah who would shelter them, hide them, and redeem them. But they did not get the message! When He came to earth, their vile corruptions raised their heads. Unbelief dragged the Jews down to earth's mire. So they "killed the Prince of life" and, in doing so, fulfilled what the prophets said they would do: pierce His hands and feet, and make Him a curse by hanging Him on a tree. It was all written—even the minutest detail of His sufferings and death—in the pages and predictions of the Old Testament.

> Now I have found the ground wherein
>   Sure my soul's anchor may remain;
> The wounds of Jesus for my sin,
>   Before the world's foundation slain;
> Whose mercy shall unshaken stay,
> When Heaven and earth are fled away.
>
> O Love, Thou bottomless abyss,
>   My sins are swallow'd up in Thee;
> Cover'd is my unrighteousness,
>   Nor spot of guilt remains on me;
> While Jesus' blood, through earth and skies,
> Mercy, free, boundless mercy, cries.

CHARLES WESLEY

16

THE CROSS IN THE LAW, THE PROPHETS, AND THE PSALMS

All things . . . were written in the law of Moses, and in the prophets, and in the psalms, concerning Me (Luke 24:44).

In this Scripture, our Lord apparently accepts the divisions of Scripture, made by the learned men of Israel, into three sections. The Law comprises the Pentateuch, the first five books written by Moses; the Prophets comprise all the major and minor prophets with the exception of Daniel; and the Psalms, or Writings, include the remainder.

The word of our Lord was that all the parts of the Old Testament spoke of His sufferings and death (Luke 24:25-27, 44). Happy are they who gather wisdom from these laden branches. The main lesson all the way through God's Book is Christ. He is the heartblood of Holy Writ. Each of these three parts seems to emphasize one aspect of our Lord's sufferings, but we must be careful not to overemphasize this. It may not be wholly so, but the emphasis is there.

The Emphasis of the Prophets

The emphasis of the prophets is our Lord's sufferings in relation to sin. The prophets speak much of sin as the abominable thing which God hates. "I hate, I despise your feast days, and I will not smell in your solemn assemblies," cried the Lord through Amos (5:21). "Will the LORD be pleased with thousands of rams, or with ten thousands of rivers of oil?" asks Micah (6:7). Not while their hands were dripping with blood, and they were oppressing the poor.

But the finest exposition relating to sin, and to the substitutionary sacrifice for sin is Isaiah 53:4-6, where the prophet mentions these seven things borne by our Lord: (1) "He hath borne our griefs," (2) "He hath . . . carried our sorrows," (3) "He was wounded for our transgressions," (4) "He was bruised for our iniquities," (5) "the chastisement of our peace was upon Him," (6) "with His stripes we are healed," (7) "the LORD hath laid on Him the iniquity of us all."

Thus, says the prophet, "He is brought as a lamb to the slaughter," that through His sacrifice sin might be taken away. In Him, His people suffer unto death. In Him, they exhaust the cup of wrath. In Him, they pay the uttermost farthing in the scales of justice. In Him, they endure until each attribute of God requires no more.

The prophets tell this out as God's plan of salvation from the beginning. The promised Redeemer is willing to come and bear all for us. He will come in the flesh. When justice in God demands man's life for his sins, the Lord Jesus answers, "I am of his nature; here is My life for his!" As the

Son of man He would have a human life to lay down—and He laid it down. He would have blood to shed—and He shed it for the ransom of us all. That is the emphasis of the prophets.

The Emphasis of the Psalms

The emphasis in the Psalms is on the sufferings and death of the Lord Jesus in relation to God. There is a great deal of detail in the Psalms about His physical sufferings, but the chief emphasis is His God-forsakenness. "My God, My God, why hast Thou forsaken Me?" (Psalm 22:1) is the epitome of that emphasis. Here is the ultimate expression of the grace of God. By substitution He appears as defiled and disfigured by the whole accumulation of our sins. He is verily accounted, and is treated, as the perpetrator of every evil deed, as the speaker of every evil word, as the harborer of every evil thought which has stained us all.

When the Lord Jesus thus appeared before God—"made . . . sin for us, who knew no sin" (2 Corinthians 5:21), then God, who is most holy, had perforce to turn His face, and the fellowship between Him and His beloved Son, as Son of man, was breached. Many martyrs have died cruel deaths and have been upborne in their sufferings by a plenitude of special and sufficient grace, but no such help could God give to His own beloved One. It was this which cut our Lord the most. This was the real heart of all His sufferings.

The Emphasis in the Law

The emphasis in the law is on the sufferings and death of our Lord in relation to faith. There are many pictures of the Redeemer's death in the first five books of the Bible: the coat of skins to cover the nakedness of Adam and Eve, Abel's sacrifice, the smitten rock, the brazen serpent, the red heifer, and all the blood sacrifices of the Mosaic ritual.

But the emphasis is always that these are to be used in order to make them effective unto salvation. The coat of skins must be put on—believingly! Israelites must strike blood upon the posts and lintels of their houses on passover night, and shelter beneath it—believingly! The wanderers in the wilderness must look to the brazen serpent to be healed—believingly! They must always look beyond the Mosaic ritual and peer down the telescope of time to see Christ and Him crucified and have personal faith in Him.

Faith is the only key to unlock the benefits of that substitutionary sacrifice. There must be more than outward ceremonial acting. There must be an inward trust in Christ. One who approaches must be aware of the holiness of God, and that vile nature must indeed shrink from His presence—that heaven must be hell to him.

But when he believes in the Lord Jesus and His sacrifice on the cross, then the Holy Spirit dethrones his love of sin, takes the barren hardness out of him, and implants a new nature which delights God. Being clothed in purple and fine linen will not do! Having power to rule vast empires and command great armies will not do! Being fair and beautiful will not do! Belonging to a church fellowship, though it be pure and simple and Biblical, will not do! Living under the blaze of eloquent gospel preaching, will not do! Having the privileges of a Christian home and upbringing will not do!

Faith alone can make the sacrifice of Christ effectual in us unto salvation. Let there be faith in Christ and Him crucified—Christ embraced as personal Saviour—and Christ is yours, and Christ is salvation.

> O blessed, living Lord,
>   Engage our hearts with Thee,
> And strike within some answering chord
>   To love so rich and free!
>
> To know Thy loving heart!
>   To cleave to Thy blest side!
> To gaze upon Thee where Thou art,
>   And in Thy love abide.
>
> Be this our one desire!
>   Thyself our object here!

The goal to which our hearts aspire—
To meet Thee in the air!

JAMES BOYD

17

THE ALMIGHTY PURGER OF SINS

His Son . . . by Himself purged our sins (Hebrews 1:2-3).

The Epistle to the Hebrews is great and profound and marvelously methodical. The first chapters are about the Person of the Lord Jesus and who He is—a Messenger of a more exalted dignity and a Minister of a more abundant grace than any before. Chapter 1 presents Him as the Divine Son of God; chapter 2 as the perfect Son of man, made like unto His brethren. These two chapters are the foundations upon which all Christian truth rests. Upon this foundation is built the whole structure of redemption.

Who the Lord Is

The opening verses tell us that God has "in these last days spoken unto us by His Son"—His unique Son—His eternal Son. There is an eternal Sonship in the Godhead. That Divine Sonship is a Sonship which belongs to the deity of the Lord Jesus Christ. Immediately following this statement about God's unique Son, there is a sevenfold exposition of His Person and His absolute and certified deity. Here are seven elements:

(1) "Heir of all things," which includes everything in the whole universe. No created being could be such an heir of this vast and illimitable universe. Only the Son of God could be that!

(2) "By whom also He made the worlds"—the "worlds" meaning the ages. The Son of God framed and designed all the ages of time and eternity. This language could not possibly be applied to any created creature!

(3) "Who being the brightness of His glory"—the clear shining of all that God is. He embodies, as in one constellation, every divine perfection. He shines with the midday splendor of Jehovah's attributes. It would be blasphemous to use such language of a mere creature!

(4) "The express image of His person"—the exact impress of God's essential nature. He was as pure on earth as God in Heaven. The Lord Jesus passed through a world of sin, as an undefilable sunbeam through the vilest hovel. He never knew sin's stain. He was as holy as God is holy because He is God!

(5) "Upholding all things by the word of His power"— keeping the whole universe in its orbit. Scientists now measure the distance of stars by sound waves rather than light years. They tell us that light from some stars takes millions of years to reach earth. They have also discovered one star bigger than our whole solar system put together. What vastness! What billions of stars there are!—and the Lord Jesus upholds them all!

What the Lord Did

(6) "By Himself purged our sins"—taking them quite away. Only because of who He is could there be a boundless substitution which could release the souls of men. Only God could bear such a load of sin, absorb all the punishment for all sins, and shed blood so meritorious and divine that it could utterly purge all sin.

We are not to forget who He is if we would rightly assess what He has done. Stand beside the cross. The sufferer on that middle cross seems a lonely man. Scorn and ridicule have been flung at Him. Affliction has marred His visage "more than any man." Verily He is man. If it were otherwise, He could possess no human blood. But is He only man? No, oh, no!

In that frail body on the cross, Deity is encased. He is the Mighty God. He is the grand Creator, sovereign Ruler over all worlds, whether of angels, men, or demons—Lord of all creation. Jehovah's plenitude of power is in His hands. Jehovah's every glory is His right. Jehovah's everlasting being is His age. Godhead is His property. Deity is linked to all His sufferings in the flesh, to all His doings in our room and stead. That blood, then, is no ordinary blood. The life is in the blood—and His life is God's life. It is the blood of God (Acts 20:28).

The shedding of this blood is boundless in its efficacy. Our sins sentence us most justly to an eternal hell since they have an infinity of claims upon us. If myriads of angels in man's form could die, all would fall far short of what sinful man deserves. But the Lord Jesus is God. He brings blood which is essentially divine. That is more than sufficient to take away all sin—more than enough to take away all the sins of all mankind. There is no boundary to its efficacy.

Where the Lord Is

(7) "He . . . sat down on the right hand of the Majesty on high"—resting from work accomplished. This signals a complete work. Here is dignity as well as grace. Here is acceptance of Him by the Father to the very throne of Heaven—and that as the Son of man, for He ascended in our manhood. Here is authority—the authority of supreme regalism. Here is the omnipotence of power, for He sits on the Father's right hand. Behold Him! See who He is, what He did, where He is!

He is God without to save us, God within to cheer us, God above to bless us, God who came in flesh and blood to die, God who reigns on the throne of Heaven to help us. He loves as God. He aids as God. He saves as God. The fullness of the Godhead is in Him.

> Crown Him with many crowns,
>   The Lamb upon His throne;
> Hark! how the heavenly anthem drowns
>   All music but its own!

Awake, my soul, and sing
  Of Him who died for thee;
And hail Him as thy matchless King
  Through all eternity.

Crown Him the Lord of years,
  The Potentate of time;
Creator of the rolling spheres,
  Ineffably sublime:
All hail, Redeemer, hail!
  For Thou hast died for me:
Thy praise shall never, never fail
  Throughout eternity.

MATTHEW BRIDGES and
GODFREY THRING

18

THE TAKING AWAY OF SINS

Christ was once offered to bear the sins of many (Hebrews 9:28).

We are sanctified through the offering of the body of Jesus Christ once for all (Hebrews 10:10).

He . . . offered one sacrifice for sins for ever (Hebrews 10:12).

By one offering He hath perfected for ever them that are sanctified (Hebrews 10:14).

The law given to Moses prescribed many sacrifices. The one of special value was a once-a-year offering on the day of atonement. If these sacrifices had been able to pacify conscience, they would not have ceased (Hebrews 10:1-2). They had, however, the very opposite effect. They brought sin to remembrance every year. The only sacrifice which could effectually remove sin and blot it out was our Lord's sacrifice of Himself on Calvary's cross. He alone is God's appointed Lamb of sacrifice, accepted of God for that end.

The Conditions for the Taking Away of Sins

The matter is of great importance. The blood of bulls and goats could not effect this. But sin had to be taken away if man was to be saved and restored to God. If God were to allow sin to go unpunished, His own honor would be lost. The eternal death of the sinner was necessary to clear the holy character of God. How, then, could the salvation of sinful man harmonize with the holy character of God? The answer is that sin must be taken away. But the blood of bulls and of goats could not do this. Thus it was that God sent His own beloved Son to do what none other could do.

First, the Lord Jesus was made subject to the law of God. The law of God was first written on the tables of men's hearts. It demanded obedience—a creature must obey his Creator! God cannot be, save on the throne of rule over His created ones. Death—eternal death—was the penalty of transgression. Adam proved a tottering reed, and the command given to test him was broken. From him, all the human race receives the spirit of disobedience.

To save man, God could not relax the requirements of His holy law—for the law of the Lord is perfect, and death is the righteous penalty of broken law. But in the fullness of time "God sent forth His Son . . . made under the law" (Galatians 4:4). He came under His own law and kept the whole of it intact. Thus He proved the law honorable—holy, just, and good.

Secondly, He bore the penalty of broken law. "Death passed upon all men," so that "in Adam all die"—all generations being in his loins. But taking away our sins was the work for which the Son of God was born in Bethlehem, lived on earth, died at Calvary, descended into the grave, rose again from the dead, mounted to Heaven, and now sits at the right hand of God. By such, our Lord became Surety for the guilty. In His sufferings and death the law was magnified and the penalty it imposed was fully paid. Thus the law can no longer accuse those who are in Christ.

Thirdly, He fulfilled the whole law. Man had dishonored God's law. It was necessary, therefore, that man should fulfill all its righteousness before God could restore him to favor. This, too, was accomplished in His dear Son. Thus He is able, not only to take away sin, but also to clothe the sinner with His own perfect righteousness. This is the robe of righteousness which now covers a true believer. It is this which beautifies and adorns his naked soul.

"There is one God, and one mediator between God and men, the man Christ Jesus; Who gave Himself a ransom for all" (1 Timothy 2:5-6). This mediation—this channel of communication—is founded on the work of atonement. The Lord Jesus is able "to bring us to God" because He "gave Himself a ransom for all."

His blood has purchased us and delivered us from hell; His righteousness buys all Heaven, and clothes us to stand in Heaven perfect before God. His righteousness is the only robe fit for such a holy place. All His redeemed ones are made beauteous in holiness. All shine in purity. All are white in spotless perfection. The eye of God rests on each with pure delight. He finds no blemish in them. They are counted worthy to sit on thrones of glory.

The Consolation in the Taking Away of Sins

The consolation of believers rests in our Lord's eternal priesthood. In Hebrews 10:10 we see believers are sanctified or set apart. The means to effect that separation is the sacrifice of our Lord Jesus—a sacrifice done "once for all."

The writer to the Hebrews goes on to show that the priests of Jewry stood—stood daily—and offered the same sacrifices. The reason for the repetition was that the blood of bulls and of goats could not take away sin. But our Lord's sacrifice was "once for all" and "for ever"—after which He "sat [down] on the right hand of God" in token of redemption completed.

There is need in salvation for the sinner to have his sins remitted and his heart cleansed, and this can be effected only through the sacrifice of Christ. "To Him give all the prophets witness, that through His name whosoever believeth in Him shall receive remission of sins" (Acts 10:43). His remission is everlasting. There is, through our Lord, not only pardon of sins but moral cleansing. Without this, we would return to folly, and it would be impossible to do that and still keep God's favor. He therefore sanctifies those who are forgiven.

Finally, under the old dispensation there were altars, priests, sacrifices—the Holy Spirit "thus signifying, that the way into the holiest of all was not yet made manifest" (Hebrews 9:8)—that sin had not been taken away. But in this new dispensation we need no altars, no priests, no sacrifices—the Holy Spirit signifying by this change that sin has been taken away and is never to be remembered, that is, no altar, but Christ; no priest, but Christ; no sacrifice, but Christ!

No blood, no altar now,
   The sacrifice is o'er!
No flame, no smoke ascends on high,
   The lamb is slain no more,
But richer blood has flowed from nobler veins,
To purge the souls from guilt, and cleanse the reddest stains.

We thank Thee for the blood,
   The blood of Christ, Thy Son:
The blood by which our peace is made,
   Our victory is won:
Great victory o'er hell, and sin, and woe,
That needs no second fight, and leaves no second foe.

HORATIUS BONAR

19

IMMEASURABLE SUFFERINGS

My God, My God, why hast Thou forsaken Me?
(Psalm 22:1)

Behold, and see if there be any sorrow, like unto My
sorrow (Lamentations 1:12).

There is nothing in the whole of human literature more
poignant than Psalm 22. It is the ultimate depth of suffering—
a prophetic portrayal of the pouring out of our Lord's soul
unto death. This psalm was committed to "the chief singer,"
as the title indicates, for none but he could have charge of
such a holy strain. The "Aijeleth Shahar" in the title is interpreted as "the hind of the morning"—a figure of Christ, the
promised Messiah. It is another portrayal of our Lord under
the figure of this gentle animal being pursued and hunted by
ferocious beasts.

It is a psalm of the cross, and expresses in detail, as nowhere else, the sufferings of our Lord on that shameful tree.
There is no psalm like this psalm. One of its most remarkable
features is the absence of any confession of sin. The sufferer
has no personal sin to be confessed, and this because it points
to the sinless Son of God as Son of man.

There are a number of beasts mentioned.

There are "bulls" in verse 12. The bull was a ceremonially
clean animal, and no doubt this points to the Jewish rulers—
scribes and Pharisees, high priests such as Annas and Caiaphas,
and the whole Jewish Sanhedrin council which plotted to put
Jesus to death.

Verse 20 speaks of "dogs." The dog was an unclean
animal and this no doubt refers to the Gentiles—often spoken

of as "Gentile dogs" by the Jews. Rome was in charge of Palestine at the time of our Lord's death, and He was condemned by the Roman governor, Pilate, to die a Roman death. Roman soldiers, too, circled the cross and gambled for His garments.

Verse 21 speaks of "lions," also unclean animals, and probably points to all the hosts of hell as ferocious and fearful enemies. They were to fling themselves upon the Lord in His moment of greatest physical weakness in the hope of tearing Him to pieces.

Then, in verse 21, the "unicorn" is mentioned, and scholars have interpreted this as the single-horned rhinoceros. It is likely a representation of death itself and its enormous power to impale men.

The Utter Dereliction of Our Lord

The first source of our Lord's sufferings was in relation to God: "My God, My God, why hast Thou forsaken Me?" (verse 1)—or, "Why hast Thou let Me go?" or "Why hast Thou given Me over?" It is the cry of One who had been in eternal communion with God, but now finds that communion is being sundered—broken in upon. It is not a rebellious cry. It is not a cry of complaint. It is one of bewilderment. Why? The answer is really given in verse 3: "But Thou art holy." At this point of time our Lord was now "made sin for us," and was standing forward as responsible for all our sins, which were laid upon Him. Thus the Father, in His office as God, had to turn away from the sight of His Son, who was now in His office of Sin-Bearer on our behalf.

The second source of our Lord's sufferings was in relation to man. The ribald mockery of men is depicted in verses 7 and 8: "All they that see Me laugh Me to scorn: they shoot out the lip, they shake the head, saying, He trusted on the LORD that He would deliver Him." Priest and people, Jews and Gentiles, soldiers and civilians are all seen in this derisive laughter, which summed up a universal scorn for God's beloved One.

And together with this mocking ribaldry were gestures of contempt, such as the shooting out of the lip, wagging the head, and other obscene gestures. Then came what may have been the cruelest part—the taunting of His faith in God, which must have been like poisoned venom to His holy soul.

The third source of our Lord's sufferings was in relation to the powers of hell. Satan marshaled all his forces and cleverly waited before attack until our Lord was brought into the most bitter extremity of physical pain: "All My bones are out of joint." It is said, I believe, that there are two hundred and eight bones in the body, and who can measure this kind of suffering when all were dislocated? It was at this strategic hour that Satan flung all his forces against Christ, hoping to overwhelm Him.

The Glorious Jubilation of Our Lord

From that deep and dire dereliction the psalm passes into the triumph of the Saviour, and thus into a paean of praise. I will mention three wondrous results from the Lord Jesus having borne our sufferings:

(1) The creation of a gospel for sinful men—a gospel of redeeming love. "I will declare Thy name unto My brethren" (verse 22)—that is, the name of God, who is just. Through the sufferings of the cross the just God found the righteous means of becoming "the justifier of him which believeth in Jesus" (Romans 3:26). Here, too, the church of firstborn ones comes into view, when the Redeemer says, "In the midst of the congregation will I praise Thee" (Psalm 22:22). He leads the praise of His redeemed ones before God the Father.

(2) The provisions of a complete satisfaction for such believing people. "The meek shall eat and be satisfied: they shall praise the LORD that seek Him: your heart shall live for ever" (verse 26). They who believe are meek in that they have renounced all human pride, and have sought after the Saviour until they found Him.

(3) The fruition of our Lord's passion gathered from all nations. "All the ends of the world shall remember and turn unto the LORD: and all the kindreds of the nations shall worship before Thee" (verse 27). They shall remember, return,

and revere the Lord.

The last phrase of the psalm is for the glory of God: "He hath done this" (verse 31), which, I understand, is but one word in Hebrew—"finished." This has reference, not only to the completed work on the cross, but to the completed work in believers as they are finally presented to the Father "without spot, or wrinkle, or any such thing"—a work wrought out to perfection in all who believe.

> Mercy and truth unite,
> O 'tis a wondrous sight,
>   All sights above!
> Jesus the curse sustains!
> Guilt's bitter cup He drains!
> Nothing for us remains,
>   Nothing but love.
>
> Love that no tongue can teach,
> Love that no thought can reach:
>   No love like His.
> God is its blessed source,
> Death can ne'er stop its course,
> Nothing can stay its force;
>   Matchless it is.

THOMAS KELLY

20

THE ACCOMPLISHED MYSTERY

My meat is to do the will of Him that sent Me, and to finish His work (John 4:34).

It is finished (John 19:30).

The Bible is God's spiritual paradise. In this paradise of God believers love to sit down in those choice spots which are thickset with the Saviour's love—where they drink from everlasting springs, where they feed on the regaling fruit of everlasting redemption.

The mystery of the Saviour's cross is too profound for us fully to understand. But there is a wondrous perfection and glory in it which satisfies the whole character of God. It is a finished work—not merely done, but perfectly done—absolutely and totally accomplished. In His final moments on the cross, the Lord Jesus was fully conscious that His cross-work had been perfect in its operation, and that its purpose had been fully achieved.

The Fact Accomplished

The Lord Jesus had been sent by the Father to do a particular work. That work was not to deal with the circumference of things—the ills of society—but to deal with the central cause of all those ills, which is sin. Nothing could remove sin but His death on the cross. From His wounded side and pierced hands, from the cross on which He died, from the altar on which He made atonement, there was to flow blood which was to do just that!

That blood was so mighty in its efficacy—so cleansing in its power—that it would wash away every speck and stain of iniquity. His great sacrifice thus became a fathomless ocean of merit which all men everywhere could freely use, and in which all their sins would disappear forever.

This is what the Lord Jesus accomplished on Calvary's cross. He dealt with the fact and issues of sin, broke the chains which bound men, and delivered men from that final end of sin which is hell.

No believer can now be given over to Satan. He owes no debt since the Lord has discharged all debt. He cannot receive the wages of wrath because they have been paid by His great Surety in his stead. He cannot be kept out of Heaven because the Lord Himself has clothed him with a robe of divine righteousness. He may advance to the very throne of God, and there he will find God's acceptance of him. He is free to be one of the citizenry of Heaven. All this is an accomplished fact.

The Office Fulfilled

The Lord Jesus was God's sent Messiah—the Christ, the Son of the living God. Three titles were bound up in this title of Messiah, and all were fulfilled in God's beloved Son.

He is the Prophet—the One who is the eternal Word of God, and who, therefore, speaks to us with absolute authority: "Verily, verily, I say unto you!" When He speaks, it is with finality. Nothing can be added. Nothing He ever said has had to be corrected or improved. The Lord never used such words as "perhaps" or "maybe." Whether He was speaking of God, of man, or redemption, or death, or eternity, or what is after death, or whatever—His were the words of absolute knowledge—the words of divine omniscience.

He is the Priest—"the one mediator between God and men" (1 Timothy 2:5). Sin had alienated men and destroyed fellowship with God. To become the true Priest, the Lord must needs offer sacrifice for sin and remove it by full atonement. And sins were a mighty load! Could He sustain them? The claims of justice formed a long roll. Could Jesus pay all? Indeed He could!—for in Him "dwelleth all the fulness of the Godhead bodily" (Colossians 2:9). Sin called for expiation. No sinner could approach a sin-hating God without a sin-removing sacrifice. Jesus became such a Priest with such an offering.

The Blessing Bestowed

The cross has a threefold blessing.

First, it delivers from sin. Sin was man's ruin. It drove man from happy fellowship with his Maker. It changed a loving child into a hardened rebel. It made the heart of man a nest of unclean birds, a spring of impure streams, a whirlpool of tumultuous passions, a hotbed of ungodly lusts. But the cross has overcome sin and made possible "the forgiveness of sins" (Ephesians 1:7). Sin has no more dominion over those who are saved by the Lord. They are no more its slaves.

Secondly, the cross delivers from shame. Sin not only bowed man down, but it filled him with shame. As soon as Adam sinned, he hid from the presence of the Lord. He was ashamed to meet God—ashamed to stand in the light of His holiness. But the cross of Christ lifts up our head so that we may say, "In the Lord have I righteousness." Such a believer can knock at Heaven's door without a blush, and with an irrefutable plea.

Thirdly, the cross delivers from sorrow. Sin brought many cares to man, and made woman to lie down in many sorrows. The fact of trials—afflictions, sickness, pain, suffering, and death—has driven many into deep depression and despair. But through the cross, such things have been transformed into purifying and sanctifying agents—tools to sharpen and polish believers as stones for the New Jerusalem. Through the cross, sorrow can now become blessed sorrow, and in it we have the soft and tender comfort of our Lord's consoling grace.

> Awake, my soul, to joyful lays,
> And sing thy great Redeemer's praise:
> He justly claims a song from me,
> His loving-kindness, oh, how free!
>
> He saw me ruined by the fall,
> Yet loved me, notwithstanding all;
> He saved me from my lost estate,
> His loving-kindness, oh, how great!
>
> When trouble, like a gloomy cloud,
> Has gathered thick and thundered loud,
> He near my soul has always stood,
> His loving-kindness, oh, how good!

SAMUEL MEDLEY

21

THE PROPITIATION FOR SINS

> Herein is love, not that we loved God, but that He
> loved us, and sent His Son to be the propitiation for our
> sins (1 John 4:10).

When a man comes before the Lord, he must do so with
humility, faith, and love. He must come full of self-abasement.
He must abhor himself. He must know that he is a lost, ruined,
undone sinner. He must see that eternal rejection is his due.
He must feel that he has no power to help himself. He must
be full, too, of sanctifying love. He cannot trust in mercy so
full—unmerited, suitable, effectual—without feeling that,
being thus purchased from perdition, he must live a willing
sacrifice to God.

But there is very much of Cain religion in the world, and
we must beware of it. Self-will is at its root. Some there are
who believe in God, and seem to come to God, but they bring,
as Cain did, the fruit of their own toil. The appearance is
fair; but the disguise eventually falls, and we see that they
are "of that wicked one." God has ordained the way, but the
self-willed and self-opinionated want a religion more suitable
to the dignity of man. They therefore grope in their own
conceits. It is the delusion of many. Professing themselves to
be wise, they become fools. Self-will, shot through with pride,
first makes a god, then a religion, then a pit of destruction
for such people.

Man's Need of a Propitiation

Man is a moral being and accountable to God. Having
sinned, he needs a propitiatory sacrifice. He has broken the

law which is "holy, just, and good." That moral law is divine in its origin, immutable in its nature, and reasonable in its requirements. The principle which refuses to obey God's law is essentially evil. Therefore, persons who breech the law must be punished. This being the case, a man can be saved only through a propitiatory offering—an atoning sacrifice—a substitution offered in his stead.

Sinful man cannot expiate his own offenses. All his good works, sufferings, austerities, and sacrifices cannot atone for a single sin. Even repentance cannot expiate sin. So man cannot provide his own propitiation. We must never close our eyes to sin's intense malignity and to the fact that it is an abomination to God, most holy.

Divine justice is inflexible. God's justice supports His own holy law, honors that law, enforces that law. If man deserves punishment for breaking the law, then justice must inflict the punishment, either upon him personally or upon a substitute. Were this not so, the moral government of the universe would break down.

God's Provision of a Propitiation

No creature could ever make propitiation for himself (that would put God under obligation to give him a reward)—present merit to God, demand justification as a reward of his good conduct. A sinful man possesses no passport into God's holy presence. He has no fit raiment for that royal court. Ignorance of this is the dark veil which blinds our race.

The Lord Jesus, God's eternal Son, is the only one who could adapt to such a propitiation. In order to become that, He had perforce to be made flesh and assume our manhood. In doing that, He united in Himself both the divine and human natures, and thus became qualified to bear what no man could ever bear. Through Him the law is magnified—made honorable—and is fully satisfied. Every claim of justice is met by Him.

We must realize that all man's own moral principles—all longings to be pure, all sense of shame—are as weak as feathers to stay a flood. He cannot stand. But through our Lord's propitiation, with His precious blood streaming to atone, a new force enters.

Man is made strong by a new life. He is set free from sin and, by the gift of Christ's own life, he rises to reign in life. The hands of the Lord Jesus have wrought a royal robe for him. The Lord Himself covers believers with a righteousness divine. God's eyes desire no more. A new man rises in Christ, and righteousness and true holiness lift up their fruitful and fragrant heads on him again.

God's Love in Providing a Propitiation

We are not to suppose for a moment that the sacrifice of the beloved Son of God was to quench the anger of the Father. That is blasphemy! Nor are we to suppose that our Lord Jesus Christ died to make God merciful. The Father, the Son, and the Holy Spirit are three Persons in the unity of the Godhead, and all act in concert.

This sacrifice to make propitiation for sins is unparalleled in its nature. It is contrary to man's own desire. It was never in man's mind to conceive such a thing. No man ever invited God to make atonement. It is "not that we loved God." It is that "He loved us, and sent His Son to be the propitiation for our sins."

Think how much God loved us! What awesome majesty is His! What high dignity belongs to God! But in order to become a satisfactory propitiation, what degradation He had to undergo, what suffering He had to endure, what shame He had to bear!

Can we not see, then, that God's great love is infinite and immense in its extent? It encompasses every age of man. It stretches throughout every race and condition. It reaches down to man in the lowest condition of human experience. It appeals to the basest and most abominable specimens of humanity. Jesus saves by rescuing from hell. Jesus saves by giving title to Heaven. Jesus saves by making man meet for Heaven. The end is surely most glorious.

How wonderful it all is! It is great because such propitiation has been willed, planned, and accepted by God, the Father; because it has been wrought out and finished by God, the Son; and because it has been applied and made effectual in believing people by God, the Holy Spirit.

When this passing world is done,
When has sunk yon glaring sun,
When I stand with Christ on high,
Looking o'er life's history;
Then, Lord, shall I fully know—
Not till then—how much I owe.

When I stand before the throne,
Dressed in beauty not my own;
When I see Thee as Thou art,
Love Thee with unsinning heart,
Then, Lord, shall I fully know—
Not till then—how much I owe.

Chosen not for good in me;
Wakened up from wrath to flee;
Hidden in the Saviour's side;
By the Spirit sanctified:
Teach me, Lord, on earth to show,
By my love, how much I owe.

R. MURRAY McCHEYNE

22

JESUS IN THE MIDST

They crucified Him, and two other with Him, on either side one, and Jesus in the midst (John 19:18).

There are several occasions when our Lord is spoken of as being in the midst. At the age of twelve He was found in the Temple "sitting in the midst of the doctors" (Luke 2:46). According to His own promise, He is "in the midst" of those who gather in His name (Matthew 18:20). After His resurrection He came and "stood in the midst" of His disciples (Luke 24:36). In John 19:18 He is on the cross between two thieves. The discerning spiritual eye can readily envisage many scenes where this is true. Some of these truths make the gospel a seed of life, a garden of pure comfort, a textbook of redeeming love.

In the Midst of Angels and Prophets

Concerning our Lord's life of redeeming love here on earth, we read: "Which things the angels desire to look into" (1 Peter 1:12). Angels have lofty intellects, but the cross of the Lord Jesus baffles their understanding. It is beyond them. They peer, probe, search diligently, and are utterly amazed at seeing the sovereign Lord of glory in the poor garb of our human nature, at witnessing His stooping into the mystery of death—His dying so cruel a death for such undeserving rebels as we are. It simply astounds them.

Then, again, here on earth in Old Testament times there were prophets inquiring into the same mystery—"Of which salvation the prophets have inquired and searched diligently, who prophesied of the grace that should come unto you" (1 Peter 1:10). God told out His plan in figures, types, representations, and illustrations. Strong efforts were made by God to break down ignorance, to introduce pure light, to open up His way of salvation. So types and figures were profusely given. Every kind of figure was used to picture the coming Christ. The Spirit of God caused the prophets to speak thus of the Redeemer for whom they searched most diligently.

Our Lord was central—in the midst of all inquiries, both of angels above and prophets below.

In the Midst of God and Sinners

When we contemplate God in His majesty, we see upon His head the crown of pure and holy excellence. He is a just

God. In His hand is an immeasurable roll, written within and without against us. It records all our sins. God would cease to be a just God if there were in Him any connivance with evil. Justice in His nature must demand that we pay what we owe.

The sinner has nothing with which to pay. We have nothing of our own but sin. Our attempt at payment would never lessen the vast amount of debt we owe for all our sins, no more than the removal of a daily grain would wear out the ocean sands.

The Lord Jesus comes in the midst of God and sinners, and in one sum discharges the whole debt. The claim against us ceases. The prisoner goes free. Justice revels in the cross, and God and man are reconciled through His blood shed there. The Saviour puts His hand on both God and man, and the gulf which separated them is spanned by Him.

In the Midst of the Old and New Covenants

The old covenant was a covenant of works. Man did not place that covenant in his heart but under his feet. He touched it only to break it and scatter it to the winds. The privileges under that covenant were instantly forfeited. We are not to dream idle dreams, as some do, that this covenant of works still lives, and that man can live through it and be justified by it. That is a broken reed—a foundation of sand.

The new covenant is a roll of divine blessings. It is clearly set forth in Jeremiah 31:33-34. It includes for the believer sanctification of spirit, adoption into God's family, divine light, and eternal pardon. The believer may claim all these as God's covenant pledge. But how can God, who is so high and so holy, whose very being is all perfection, whose home is eternity, contract with man who is so low, so vile, so loathsome—the offspring of all corruption?

The answer is that the Lord Jesus is in the midst. The covenant rests upon His work. It is written in unfading letters of eternal love, and is based upon God's unchangeable purpose in His Son. It is made with Jesus as our Representative. He stands in the midst.

In the Midst of Friends and Foes

Friends were few at the cross. John, Mary Magdalene, Mary the mother of Jesus, and another, were about all that were left—a few friends who loved Him. There was a tremendous breakdown of human nature at the cross, and few there were who saw the Lord's dying love, and His blood streaming to atone for human sin.

His foes were many. The priests were full of hate because of the Lord's rebuke about their making clean the outside of the platter and because of His inveighing against their useless ceremonials which were mere play-acting. Pilate was wilting under fear of his master, Caesar, afraid of losing his job and the political goodwill of the Jews. Herod the king was mocking—a carnal, adulterous "fox," as the Lord called him. The crowd was superficial—those who had cried "hosanna" were now crying "crucify" as though He were the basest of all. The soldiers—hardened gamblers—were at the foot of the cross, throwing dice for His vestments.

But Jesus is in the midst, and because He is, some, like the centurion, will cross from the company of His foes to the circle of His friends.

In the Midst of Saved and Damned

When Joseph was in prison two notable offenders were by his side. Human judgment discerned no difference. Both had offended. They were involved in Pharaoh's displeasure, and both expected an ignominious end. But one mounts the path of favor and is crowned with honors, the other is left in bonds to perish (Genesis 40).

This is a signal to the distant wonders of the cross. There is a corresponding circumstance. Two thieves are crucified, one on either side of our Lord. But as they writhe in torment, Jesus is in the midst. A change takes place in one— as great as light from darkness, life from death. He loathes the sin which he had fondled. He confesses its malignity. He looks to Jesus and cries: "Lord, remember me!" that is, "Lord, I am perishing. Thou only canst save me!" And saved he is! "To day shalt thou be with Me in paradise." The other perishes—hardened by his sufferings. Hell was near, but he neither saw, nor feared, nor shunned it.

> Jesus! That name is Love,
>   Jesus, our Lord!
> Jesus, all names above,
>   Jesus, the Lord!
> Thou, Lord, our all must be;
> Nothing that's good have we,
> Nothing apart from Thee,
>   Jesus, our Lord!
>
> Righteous alone in Thee,
>   Jesus, the Lord!
> Thou wilt a refuge be,
>   Jesus, our Lord!
> Whom then have we to fear,
> What trouble, grief, or care,
> Since Thou art ever near?
>   Jesus, our Lord!

JAMES G. DECK

23

LOVE AND RIGHTEOUSNESS IN THE CROSS

Whom God hath set forth . . . to declare His righteousness (Romans 3:25).

Hereby perceive we the love of God, because He laid down His life for us (1 John 3:16).

In the days when our Lord was here on earth, the cross was a Roman means of death. But the Roman, who devised it, did not like to write about it, think about it, hear about it, or talk about it. The cross was abhorrent to the Roman. The victim was associated with evil, and represented a degraded and disgraceful specimen of humanity. The cross was looked upon as associated with ignominy, crime, and weakness.

But the cross of the Lord Jesus changed that! His cross was neither an accident nor a mere expression of the malice of men. It was a God-planned cross—His plan for human redemption. Since it is by works we express what we are, then, since the cross is God's greatest work, it must be the greatest revelation of His character.

The apostles gloried in the cross—in our Lord's cross. Since it wrought redemption for fallen man, it became the symbol of life, hope, and blessing. It is at His cross that fallen man hears the joyful news of salvation, a gospel unheard of in hell, but which has fallen on our ears—the sweetest melody our ears have ever heard. It is written by God's own pen in the Scriptures of truth—fixed, eternal, and divine. Every attribute of God has concurred in erecting it. There is no defect in this plan of God—no blemish—no decay.

The Cross—the Love of God

"In this was manifested the love of God toward us, because that God sent His only begotten Son into the world, that we might live through Him. Herein is love, not that we loved God, but that He loved us, and sent His Son to be the propitiation for our sins" (1 John 4:9-10). The salvation of man has come out of God's great heart of love—His unmeasured and immeasurable love.

Every stone in this edifice has been shaped by love and laid by love. The supreme expression of that infinite love is that His beloved Son came down from Heaven, was born in Bethlehem, lived in Nazareth, died at Calvary, descended into the grave, burst the bands of death, rose into Heaven, and now sits at the right hand of God. He did all that because He loved us!

There are certain experiences in human existence which have the tendency to challenge the love of God. We witness the violence in nature—the calamity of earthquakes, floods, droughts, hurricanes, pestilences—and such things afford opportunity for the evil in the heart of man to challenge God's love. Or we go through the trials of social and family life—disfiguring and crippling infirmities, prevailing and ravaging sicknesses, the incidence of poverty and misery, and finally, death—and we wonder! Does God really love us? Why has God allowed this to come to us? These things blow up the smoke of unbelief. They tend to bring to man the bitterness of despair and a sense of hopelessness in the battle of life.

But whatever challenges these things may bring, we look at the cross of God's beloved Son and know, beyond a shadow of doubt, that God loves us. In giving His Son to die for us, God gave everything He could give. He gave His all. "Hereby perceive we the love of God, because He laid down His life for us" (1 John 3:16). Here is love immeasurable in its breadth, and length, and depth, and height—"the love of Christ, which passeth knowledge" (Ephesians 3:19) as the hymn says: "Deep, vast, immeasurable, Love—profound"! "God is love."

The Cross—the Righteousness of God

"Christ Jesus: whom God hath set forth to be a propitiation . . . to declare His righteousness" (Romans 3:24-25). God is a God of law. The natural world is founded upon the Creator's governing laws. God has written moral law on the tables of the human heart. If God would save man, then salvation must answer to His own holy law. Forgiveness must be based on righteousness. However much God may love, He cannot wink at sin or fail to punish it.

When God's holy law examines God's beloved Son in His own personal life, it can find no fault in Him. He comes forth in all the glory of pure sinlessness. No cleansing is needed for Himself. Hence "the righteousness of Christ"—His own personal righteousness—is what He Himself is. Perfection finds embodiment in Him. His every aspect is righteousness—without a single flaw. He has no stain. Sin could not touch

Him. Earth witnessed in Him the sinless Son of man. His whole life on earth shone with godlike purity.

But when He stood forth to answer for our sins, to take full responsibility for them, and bear the punishment of them, then the law saw Him as a sin-laden Person, and justice thus cried: "Awake, O sword, against My shepherd, and against the man that is My fellow [equal], saith the LORD of hosts" (Zechariah 13:7). The law must now condemn Him. The law must afflict Him and put Him to grief. The law must erect a cross and hang Him on it—to be "made a curse for us" (Galatians 3:13). The law must shed His precious blood. Why? Because God is righteous, and any forgiveness must be based on righteousness, else it would never answer to the justice of God—never bring peace to conscience—never silence the accusations of Satan.

In Old Testament days, as we see in Romans 3:25, God could only cover sins in the symbolic sacrifices of Jewry, "For it is not possible that the blood of bulls and of goats should take away sins" (Hebrews 10:4). But our Lord was "the Lamb of God, which taketh away the sin of the world" (John 1:29)—even those sins which had been but covered in times past. Where are our sins now? They have been taken away where they cannot be found. Thus believers cannot be condemned. Faith in the Lord Jesus casts away all misery with one hand, and with the other grasps eternal joy and happiness.

> Jesus, Thy blood and righteousness
> My beauty are, my glorious dress;
> 'Midst flaming worlds, in these arrayed,
> With joy shall I lift up my head.

> Bold shall I stand in that great day,
> For who aught to my charge shall lay?
> Fully absolved through these I am,
> From sin and fear, from guilt and shame.

> Lord, I believe Thy precious blood,
> Which, at the mercy seat of God,

Forever doth for sinners plead,
For me, e'en for my soul, was shed.

NICOLAUS L. VON ZINZENDORF

24

WISDOM AND POWER IN THE CROSS

O the depth of the riches . . . of the wisdom . . . of God (Romans 11:33).

Christ the power of God (1 Corinthians 1:24).

The Cross—the Wisdom of God

"The preaching of the cross is to them that perish foolishness" (1 Corinthians 1:18). That wondrous cross has no charm for an unbeliever. It is a sad, sad thing that unbelief has so blinded the eyes of men that they see no beauty in the Lord Jesus that they should desire Him, and no value in His sacrifice. The altogether lovely One is not lovely to them. He who is the essence of preciousness is but vile in their sin-clouded eyes. God's grandest gift is scorned by them. Heaven's glory is cast away like "a root out of a dry ground" and as a husk to the wind.

But in the cross of Christ our Lord there is the fruit of God's omniscient mind—the mind of the all-wise God. It is the expression of the eternal thought of God which is absolute wisdom. When Paul was at Corinth, he saw that the cross was foolishness to the intellectual Greek. Pride in such men must find a way to God more suitable to the supposed dignity of man. They turn from the revealed plan and wisdom of God to grope in the darkness of their own conceits. They place their puny reason above the counsels of the Most High

God, who alone is the all-wise One.

What a delusion sin has brought to man! The intellectuals of this world's wisdom know not that all they have is unenlightened reason. No light from Heaven shines into man's darkened mind. Sin has plunged reason into the dust so that man cannot know the things of God.

Out of this unenlightened reason, pride rises up to make man walk in a vain show. He feels neither sin nor the need of pardon. Like Cain of old, he will dare to come before God with the fruit of his own toil, and proudly trample on the blood offering of the Saviour. The blood of Christ is offensive to his taste. He thinks he has need of nothing. Thus pride closes his eyes—he cannot see the Lord. It closes his heart—he will not receive Him.

Wherein, then, do we see the wisdom of God in the cross? It lies in the perfect concurrence of His love and His justice. On the one hand, God loved man and desired to save him. On the other hand, His justice required that each sin of man be punished. How then could God save man? What means could produce such a saving work?

It is here that God's wisdom is displayed in devising a means whereby "He might be just, and the justifier of him which believeth in Jesus" (Romans 3:26). His devised means is in the cross! Till this is seen, the soul of man will never see God's salvation—never see how sins are washed away—never see how the gates of hell are shut, how the door of Heaven is opened—never see and enjoy the eternal rest of God.

The Cross—the Power of God

"Unto them which are called, both Jews and Greeks, Christ the power of God" (1 Corinthians 1:24). "Unto us which are saved it is the power of God" (1 Corinthians 1:18). The cross is not just an objective display of God's love, righteousness, and wisdom. It is designed for a very practical purpose—that of saving men. It is God's means by which He can bring many sons to glory and make them eternally joyful, eternally happy, eternally peaceful.

Thus God not only gave His beloved Son and sent Him to be the Saviour of the world; not only did God's beloved Son finish and complete the work of redemption by drinking up the cup of wrath upon the deserving sin of man; but He has sent forth the Holy Spirit to knock on the barred doors of sinful man's heart. For this purpose the Holy Spirit assails the fortress of self-love, reveals the perils of sin, and points the penitent to the cross of Jesus our Lord so that he may shelter in the sure refuge of the sacrifice of the cross.

The cross is raised on earth to save men. It takes power of God to do that! There is no sin of man so crimson red but that it cannot be washed away by the precious blood of Jesus. There is no sinner so far away from God that he cannot be found and brought home again. That is the power of God! There is no remaining sin so deeply entrenched in a believer's heart that it cannot be overcome and stripped of its power.

Through the cross God gives forgiveness to the guilty, peace to the conscience-stricken, cleansing for the defiled, victory for the defeated, relief for the burdened, rest for the weary, courage to the faint, confidence to the dying, and comfort to the bereaved. The cross of Christ has all that power, and much more. It is "the power of God."

It is a thing most wonderful,
    Almost too wonderful to be,
That God's own Son should come from Heav'n
    And die to save a child like me.

I cannot tell how He could love
    A child so weak and full of sin;
His love must be most wonderful
    If He could die my love to win.

And yet I want to love Thee, Lord;
    O light the flame within my heart!
And I will love Thee more and more
    Until I see Thee as Thou art.

WILLIAM W. HOW

25

THE WORK OF THE CROSS

Now is the judgment of this world: now shall the
prince of this world be cast out. And I, if I be lifted up
from the earth, will draw all men unto Me (John 12:31-32).

In this word our Lord signified what manner of death He
would die. With the coming and inquiring of the Greeks to
see Him, the Lord answered that His hour was come that He
should be glorified, and forthwith the troubling of His soul
began. "Now is my soul troubled."

He was now facing the cross with its unutterable physical
pain and bitterest anguish of spirit. The peals of terrifying awe
were beginning to ring in His ears. The Man of Sorrows was now
to taste the bitter cup and give up Himself—His life, His blood—
to make His soul an offering for sin. But this was the cause for
which He had come into the world, and there was no other
response from His heart of love than to say, "Father, glorify
Thy name" (John 12:28). "Then came there a voice from heav-
en, saying, I have both glorified it, and will glorify it again."

The Discerning Power

"Now is the judgment of this world." Men by nature
are lovers of pleasure, worshipers of its god, admirers of its
vanity, indulgers of its flesh. But the world, with its maxims
and principles and fashions is judged by the cross. The love
of the world—its foolish vanities, its empty shows, its godless
maxims, its defiling pleasures, its lying principles, its soul-
beclouding books, and all its idolatrous worship of talent,
wit, and falsely called glory—is condemned by the cross of
Christ. The Lord's own discerning eye saw and described its

real character. Its nectar is poison and must be avoided. Its touch is that of a viper's sting and must be shunned.

What profit would it be to hold the scepter of kingdoms, to call the whole race of men our vassals, to look upon everything in the world as private possessions, to revel in all its ease and luxury, to drink the fullest cup of its pleasures, to sit on the highest throne of its honor, to be caressed by all its affection, to be extolled by all the adulation of men if there were no cross of Christ, and thence no salvation for our souls.

This world's system was judged at the cross of our Lord Jesus Christ. In the great body called Christendom there are formalists, externalists, half-hearted Christians, and half-and-half disciples who have never broken with sin, nor separated from this vile world, nor crucified self, nor taken up the cross. Nothing can deliver from the delusion of false notions but a clear view of the cross of Christ. Once we have seen that, we will despise the world which crucified Him.

The Destructive Power

"Now shall the prince of this world be cast out." Behind all flesh and blood is the infernal world of Satan and all his hosts—the real driving force behind the sinful acts of man. In the conflict of the cross, Satan showed his total strength, but how could he match the Son of God? Our Lord went to the cross as a conqueror over Satan. He entered into death as into the citadel of the enemy's entrenched power, to strip him of that power and make men free to rise out of its enslavement.

The actual victory over this ancient and powerful foe was accomplished, not in the resurrection, but in the cross. The resurrection demonstrated that victory, but the victory itself was wrought out on the cross when our Lord flung off all the assault of hell—"And having spoiled principalities and powers, He made a shew of them openly, triumphing over them in it" (Colossians 2:15).

The devil is not annihilated. Indeed, he still reigns and rules over and controls all men outside of Christ. But the Lord rendered him inoperative against Himself and against all those who abide in Christ. He can no longer hold dominion over the redeemed in Christ—no longer bind them with his chains—no longer hold them by the power of death. That power of his has been destroyed with respect to the Son of God and His redeemed ones.

The Drawing Power

"I, if I be lifted up, will draw all men unto Me." How gloriously true! Ever since that accomplished redemption on Calvary's cross, He has drawn men from every nation, kindred, tribe, and tongue. It is not the wooden cross which is the attractive power. We must beware of the sentimentality written in such hymns as "The Old Rugged Cross." It is not the wood of the cross but the Person who was crucified on that cross who attracts—"I, if I."

Oh, how He draws! Here, where the mind and heart focus upon Christ and Him crucified, and where there is a wholehearted trust in Him, blind eyes are opened, frozen feelings melt, pride is laid low, strong prejudices give place, hearts open, and the Lord Jesus enters. On the day of Pentecost three thousand souls were saved, and so goes the story all through the two thousand years since that blessed work was accomplished.

The pages of our Bible cry: "Sin need not be the ruin of any man or woman!" Here is a Saviour lifted up who draws to Himself with cords of infinite love. He has finished transgression and made an end of sin. No second cross is required on some new Golgotha. His one cross—His one death on that cross—has presented a complete propitiation and brought redemption to our captive souls. Oh, let that lifted-up Saviour be all our praise, and that wondrous, glorious cross charm our souls forever.

> O Love that wilt not let me go,
>   I rest my weary soul in Thee;
> I give Thee back the life I owe,

That in Thine ocean depths its flow
  May richer, fuller be.

O Light that followest all my way,
  I yield my flickering torch to Thee;
My heart restores its borrowed ray,
That in Thy sunshine's blaze its day
  May brighter, fairer be.

O Cross that liftest up my head,
  I dare not ask to fly from Thee;
I lay in dust life's glory dead,
And from the ground there blossoms red
  Life that shall endless be.

GEORGE MATHESON

26

REDEMPTION THROUGH THE CROSS

In whom we have redemption through His blood, the
forgiveness of sins, according to the riches of His grace
(Ephesians 1:7).

The need for redemption and the consequent forgiveness
of sins lies in the fact that man has sinned. We all have need
of forgiveness. Sin is trangression of God's holy law, and can
be righteously forgiven only through the shed blood of Christ
our Saviour.

The sin of man is not a trivial fault, easily pardoned, easily
effaced. The slightest sin is open rebellion. It casts God down
from His throne of rule in the heart of man. It avows the godless principle of independence. It sets up self-love as an idol
in place of the living God. God is holy, and cannot connive at
evil. He abhors it. To transgress His law is death— death
which is the withdrawal of God's holy presence from man.

The Source of Redemption

The source of redemption is clearly written in the text as "the riches of His grace." We cannot secure redemption by anything which we can do. It is all of grace from beginning to end. There can be no merit of man where grace operates, or else it would make grace of none effect. Nor does grace merely supplement our deficiency—making up the measure where we may fall short. No! It is "not of works, lest any man should boast" (Ephesians 2:9). We are a sinful race—death-stricken in body, dead in soul and spirit. The life of God was extinguished in man the moment man sinned. "In Adam all die."

It is "the riches of His grace" which has wrought our redemption for us. The movement toward it began in the heart of God—the outflow of His love which, coming to such undeserving sinners, is now known as grace.

That grace is not withheld from sinful man because he lacks merit. It is given because he has no merit and because of his unworthiness. If man had any merit at all, then God would be obliged to give him a reward for this merit. But we have none, so that what God gives is all of grace. Nor is grace more to the less deserving—less grace to those who have sinned more, more grace to those who have sinned less. No! "The riches of His grace" is abundantly lavished upon all our race.

The Ground of Forgiveness

"Through His blood," says the text. The only ground upon which God could procure the forgiveness of sins was through the precious blood of His own beloved Son. Forgiveness must please and answer to the holiness, truth, righteousness, and justice of God. But the blood of Jesus is so precious, the shedding of it so meritorious, that all manner of sin can be forgiven the children of men. It makes the scarlet white as snow and the crimson like wool. It transforms the vilest into perfect purity. Its merits render and present men spotless before God.

The blood of Christ accomplishes all this. He has "by Himself purged our sins" (Hebrews 1:3). This was done on Calvary's cross and is an accomplished fact. This He did when, on that cross, He "offered up Himself" (Hebrews 7:27) and thus through His own blood "obtained eternal redemption for us" (Hebrews 9:12).

We are not to make pictures of the blood. Some of our hymns tend to do that—as, for instance, a river of blood into which we are to plunge. No! We must interpret the blood. Blood is the symbol of life. "The life of the flesh is in the blood" (Leviticus 17:11). The shedding of blood, therefore, is life poured out, and life voluntarily laid down is sacrifice. The pouring out of the Saviour's blood is the basis upon which God can grant a righteous forgiveness.

The forgiveness of sins is the profoundest of all problems. The real question is not why God finds it difficult to forgive, but how a just and holy God can forgive. The only way He can do this is through the blood of His own holy and perfect Son, and the sacrifice for sin He made on our behalf.

The Assurance of These Blessings

The text tells us that in Christ "we have redemption through His blood, the forgiveness of sins." "In whom"— that is, in Christ! Only because He is God could He redeem, and remain supported under the whole flood of God's out-poured wrath. Who but God Himself could bear that? But there is one thing we ourselves have to do—that is to believe and receive it. Believing is an act which puts us, as it were, in Christ, and in Him we have redemption and forgiveness. To be in Him is to be joined to Him—made one with Him. All spiritual blessings are in Christ, and in none other, and become ours when we are in Him.

In another Scripture we are told that "we have peace with God" (Romans 5:1)—we have it! In verse 2 "we have access"—we have it! So here—"we have redemption . . . and the forgiveness of sins"—we have them! Let us not pass by this confident assurance. This assures us that God's smile is upon us. No enmity remains. Reconciliation is complete.

Faith is not some pious hope for the future, but a present experience of every trusting soul and something consciously enjoyed. Thus we read: "If we confess our sins, He is faithful and just to forgive us our sins, and to cleanse us from all unrighteousness" (1 John 1:9)—that is, it is the right thing for God to do. Since He has promised, He is faithful to keep His promise. God cannot be unfaithful because He has promised. He cannot be unrighteous because the blood of Christ has been shed.

> Amazing grace! how sweet the sound,
>   That saved a wretch like me!
> I once was lost, but now am found;
>   Was blind, but now I see.
>
> 'Twas grace that taught my heart to fear,
>   And grace my fears relieved;
> How precious did that grace appear
>   The hour I first believed.
>
> Through many dangers, toils, and snares,
>   I have already come;
> 'Tis grace that brought me safe thus far,
>   And grace will lead me home.

JOHN NEWTON

27

FAITH—LOOKING AND PARTAKING

> As Moses lifted up the serpent in the wilderness, even so must the Son of man be lifted up: that whosoever believeth in Him should not perish, but have eternal life (John 3:14-15).

> Whoso eateth My flesh, and drinketh My blood, hath eternal life (John 6:54).

The forgiveness of sins is not enjoyed by all men. The gospel of the cross is good news to all men. It is a message of forgiveness—not through the birth, or the teaching, but through the death of the Lord Jesus. But the benefits of that sacrifice—such as forgiveness, acceptance, reconciliation, communion—are enjoyed only by those who avail themselves of those benefits, those who wholeheartedly believe in, and give themselves to, the Lord Jesus.

Such is saving faith—the faith that saves. Faith is not saving in its exercise if there is any vagueness about the Person of the Lord Jesus Christ, or if He is viewed as anything less than the Almighty God become man, who bled and died in our room and stead. True saving faith is born in Heaven; it is the brightest star in the firmament of grace. It reads the mind of God in the cross, and kindles trust and devotion in God's blessed Son. The Lord Jesus has made this faith simple to understand, both in its object and in its character.

Faith Is Looking

"As Moses lifted up the serpent in the wilderness, even so must the Son of man be lifted up." That takes us back to an event in Israel's wilderness wanderings. Israel began to loathe the manna sent down from heaven and, in doing so, despised the Son of God it typified. "Our soul loatheth this light bread," said they! Whatever God did in those days, He ever had His Son in view. God had given Israel manna from heaven in the wilderness—a wilderness which could produce no sustenance for them. The supply of life-sustaining food was wholly from above—from the God of Heaven, unseen before by human eyes, untouched by human hands. It set forth the Son of God in type in His descent into the earth as the living Bread.

But Israel loathed it though it was sweet, nourishing, and all-sufficient. For the despising of this, God judged the offense and sent fiery serpents among them, so that, when bitten, the power of death worked in them. They were condemned to death.

But God, who by reason of His own just character, must needs judge sin, also, because He is love, provided a remedy. Moses was to set up a brazen serpent on a pole as a symbol of the curse, and a type which the Lord used to describe His own lifting up on the cross to be "made sin for us."

All that God required of those Israelites who have been bitten was that they look to the uplifted serpent—not to Moses, not to the sun's rays, not to fighting the serpent—but only to the uplifted serpent. It was as simple as that! Thus we see in this figure that God has given us the remedy for sin's poison in the cross of Christ. Saving faith is looking only to Him—to Christ and Him crucified. It is "look and live"—"that whosoever believeth in Him should not perish, but have everlasting life."

Faith Is Partaking

This is the second metaphor left us by our Lord to describe saving faith. "Whoso eateth My flesh, and drinketh My blood, hath eternal life." The teaching of our Lord took the Jews back to another event in their history. The wilderness yielded no food and no drink. But they were fed by manna sent down from heaven, and they were given water to drink from the smitten rock—both types of Christ in His incarnation and in His sufferings and death. All that the hungering and thirsting Israelites had to do in the wilderness was to partake of what God had provided.

We are not to think of His flesh and blood in a carnal sense. It is not the flesh of His body in which He dwelt in Palestine which we are to eat. That is not possible and, if it were, it would be cannibalism. Also, it is not the material blood which coursed in our Lord's veins while living in His human body which we are to drink. His flesh and His blood were offered in sacrifice for sins on Calvary's cross. Faith must look to that substitutional sacrifice, which saves forever the souls of all poor sinners who accept it by faith. Through that sacrifice all manner of sin is forgiven the children of men. It cleanses from all sin. It removes all guilt. Its merits save to the utmost.

But what is faith—the faith which saves? It is like eating and drinking. When we do this in a physical way we take in something. We appropriate, use, and digest what is placed before us in the way of food and drink. It is simply accepting and using the provision made for our well-being. Such is saving faith. The sole object of saving faith is Christ and Him crucified. Faith is appropriating what He has done for our good. It is not faith in good works, not faith in baptism, not faith in the church, but faith in Christ and Him crucified.

That faith is not credulity—just believing anything of a religious character. It is not credence—accepting a certain creed of men. It is a heart experience which trusts, and takes in—appropriates—what the Lord Jesus Christ is to us in this sacrificial and substitutionary sacrifice which He made on Calvary's cross. We receive it in the same way as eating and drinking—taking in an all-sufficient, life-giving, fully satisfying feast of good things.

My faith looks up to Thee,
Thou Lamb of Calvary,
Saviour divine!

Now hear me while I pray,
Take all my guilt away,
O let me from this day
  Be wholly Thine!

May Thy rich grace impart
Strength to my fainting heart,
  My zeal inspire;
As Thou hast died for me,
O may my love to Thee
Pure, warm, and changeless be,
  A living fire!

RAY PALMER

28

THE RESURRECTION SIDE OF THE CROSS

He must go unto Jerusalem, and suffer many things...
and be killed, and be raised again the third day (Matthew
16:21).

The emphasis of the New Testament is upon the death
of the Lord Jesus, since by His death He dealt with our sins
and wrought out redemption for us. He took them quite
away. But the Christ who died, and descended into the grave,
rose again; and the Christ who rose again was the Christ who
died. Life seemed to be extinct. The grave made fast its bars.

But every foe was foiled. Death and hell yielded. The
tomb opened its portal. The mighty Conqueror strode forth
alive. He was the first fruits from among the dead.

The Resurrection Demonstrates His Deity

"And declared to be the Son of God with power, according to the spirit of holiness, by the resurrection from the

dead" (Romans 1:4). When our Lord warned His disciples that He must die, they did not understand it. Was He really the Son of God? When at last He was arrested, tried, condemned, and crucified, the disciples must have wondered. Instead of reigning over a kingdom on earth, as they supposed He would, He had suffered the shame and ignominy of crucifixion. How could He be the Son of God and allow men to kill Him? Might it be that He was not the Messiah—the Redeemer? So they may have queried!

But, then, He arose; He lives; He comes forth again to God. And in His resurrection He was powerfully declared to be the Son of God. The resurrection proved it beyond a shadow of doubt.

A very important event in the Old Testament was the throwing up of Jonah by the big fish which had swallowed him. This was a pointer to our Lord's resurrection—a type of it.

It was the resurrection which convinced Mary in the garden, which restored Peter's confidence after his threefold denial, which made doubting Thomas cry, "My Lord and my God," which revived the hopes of the two despondent disciples who were going to Emmaus, which brought new hope to the disciples who had gone back fishing and had caught nothing, and which convinced Saul of Tarsus on the Damascus Road.

The Resurrection Confirms the Efficacy of His Death

"We believe on Him that raised up Jesus our Lord from the dead; who was delivered for our offences, and was raised again for our justification" (Romans 4:24-25). When the Lord Jesus died, anxious hearts may have inquired: He came, He died to save—but may He not have failed?

The Lord Himself had foretold not only His death but the purpose of it: "to give His life a ransom for many," that His blood was to be shed for the remission of sins. But how do we know that for sure? May He not have failed? Oh, no! The resurrection proves that the purpose for which He died was accomplished. All claims were satisfied. All enemies were subdued. All the worst that hell could do against Him was now a broken reed. The resurrection was God's proof and evidence that our Lord had not died in vain. Because that purpose had been accomplished, and full satisfaction for sins had been made, God raised Him from the dead for our justification.

The Apostle Paul in 1 Corinthians 15:17-18,20, says, "If Christ be not raised, your faith is vain; ye are yet in your sins. Then they also which are fallen asleep in Christ are perished. . . . But now is Christ risen from the dead, and become the firstfruits of them that slept." So believers are no longer in their sins, but are justified from all things. Those who have died in the Lord are not perished, but are safe home with the Lord.

The Resurrection Completes
the Redemptive Work of the Cross

"For if we have been planted together in the likeness of His death, we shall be also in the likeness of His resurrection" (Romans 6:5). The resurrection of our body is part of redemption's fruit. Death, like the devil, is a conquered foe. It will come and extend its hand to take down our crumbling clay abode. It will consign the bodies of believers to a narrow cell, and worms will do their work. This body is sin-soiled and cannot be taken into God's Heaven.

But death's seeming triumph over the body is a real defeat. It wounds only to heal. It means that the body will rise in fresher beauty. Oh, how changed that body will be! It shall shine brighter than the noonday sun. It will be no longer fleshly but spiritual.

We can hardly conceive the glory of that resurrection body. But it is true and it is near. The trumpet will soon sound to call the bodies of believers to arise. The Lord of life is at the door. This is part of the blessed gospel, that we glory in resurrection hopes.

Then will the Lord display before the Father the many

members who compose His spiritual body. He pleads that
they may be gathered from the world. He offers them as consecrated for the Father's use. What a sight that will be! To
see the Saviour's nail-marked hand present our fully-redeemed
persons to God the Father!

> One day they led Him up Calvary's mountain,
> One day they nailed Him to die on the tree;
> Suffering anguish, despised and rejected:
> Bearing our sins, my Redeemer is He!
>
> One day the grave could conceal Him no longer,
> One day the stone rolled away from the door;
> Then He arose, over death He had conquered;
> Now is ascended, my Lord evermore!
>
> One day the trumpet will sound for His coming,
> One day the skies with His glories will shine;
> Wonderful day, my beloved ones bringing;
> Glorious Saviour, this Jesus is mine!

J. WILBUR CHAPMAN

29

IN REMEMBRANCE

This do in remembrance of Me (1 Corinthians 11:24).

It is an astonishing thing that we who have been redeemed
need a reminder of our Lord's death upon the cross. Yet it
is so! If we search our hearts and examine our ways, we shall
find it is easy to forget. Our Lord, who knows well the
weakness and treachery of our human hearts, has made provision for us to be constantly reminded. Thus He has estab-

lished the memorial feast with this intent, "This do in remembrance of Me."

The Lord's things are sublime in their simplicity. This feast is so—"simple bread and simple wine, sweet memorials of our Lord." Faith alone can interpret these elements and in them catch the image of our beloved Lord. Faith has learned the sound principle that natural things reflect the beauties and glories and even the sufferings of the Lord Jesus. It is seen in the elements upon the table, the testimony of the true bread and true wine, and how He became food and drink for our souls.

It is most inspiring to read church history and witness the many strange places where the saints have set up a table of sorts and used these simple memorials to remember their Lord, as, for instance, in the catacombs of Rome, in the Scottish moorlands, in concentration camps, in exiles' lonely prisons, on battlefields, yea, in every kind of place.

A Commanded Remembrance

There is the Lord's own authority for observing this feast. It is no sentimental arrangement by some specially devoted believers. In these words of our text, which had been communicated to the Apostle Paul, the permanence of this service was established. It was instituted by the Lord Himself in Matthew 26:26-28. Acts 2:42 records the first occasion of believers' obedience to His command; and in Acts 20:7 we see that it became the general practice of the church to observe this on "the first day of the week."

The words, "this do" and "as oft as," contain the idea of repetition; that the feast is to be observed again and again. It is a command, as it were, written by our Lord's own pen. It is the decree of His own mouth, the fruit of His own omniscient mind, the perfection of His thought. All He commands is surely designed by His wisdom and laid down by His grace. "I have received of the Lord," said Paul—which means a clear communication from the Lord. The observance, therefore, has never to be one of mere impulse or of natural inclination, but observed because the Lord has ordained that we should keep it.

A Visible Remembrance

The form of the remembrance matches our weakness. We need to see something to aid our faith. We must handle things. It almost seems that pure faith is so feeble in most men that we need help through the physical senses. The Lord has provided for this need and given us these elements which can be seen and handled.

The history of God's dealings with man, especially in communicating profound truth, is full of visible and tangible objects for the bodily senses to contemplate: the rainbow, the passover meal, the booths at the feast of tabernacles, the rod of Aaron, the pot of manna, the stones of witness from the river Jordan, and hundreds more.

The bread and the wine are but emblems—commemorative emblems. "This is My body"—not that the bread is His actual body, but that it represents His body. "This cup is the new testament in My blood"—not that the cup is the testament, but that the wine in it is a token of the covenant. It is metaphorical language which all of us use every day. Is not our Lord's purport clear as day? We are not to read mystical things into these simple emblems, and either make them or change them into something other than they are. They picture Christ. They are models of His saving work. They are there with one design: to set forth Christ and proclaim His redeeming love.

A Strengthening Remembrance

This remembrance feast is a means of grace. While the elements on the table are but emblems, the feast is not a bare commemoration. We rise above the elements. We gaze at our Lord Himself, and it is upon Him that our souls feed. The faith of the believer must look beyond the elements. All that our Lord is in Himself is the believer's grand portion.

Now that we are in Him, His wisdom is ours to guide; His power is ours to uphold; His faithfulness and truth are our shield and buckler; His Spirit is given us to teach, solace, and bless us; His righteousness is ours to make us walk uprightly; His Heaven is ours to be our home. It is meditation upon such blessed realities which is the strengthening portion of this feast.

A Personal Remembrance

"This do ye." Our remembrance of the Lord is more than a mere remembrance of the historical event of His dying. It is the remembrance that it was for each of us personally— for me, even me! He does not ask that we remember the date or even the place of His sacrifice, but that we remember Him. Our eyes must focus, not upon the tree (on bits of wood supposedly from His cross, or bits of the napkin once wound around His head) but upon the Lord Himself. In the same way we are not to remember the Lord's supper as a doctrine, or a precept, or an event; but we are to remember the Lord Himself. Our thought must not stray from Him. We are not to magnify a man who distributes the elements. We are not to magnify the ordinance. We are not to make superstition out of this feast. We are to remember only the Lord Jesus Himself.

A Spiritual Remembrance

This gathering to partake of the Lord's Supper is more than a ceremony. We are to come to it with spiritual affections. The spirit of the believer must be exercised. The heart must go out to Him. This means a sense of reverence and godly fear. We are to examine ourselves and so partake worthily; that is, we are to have regard to the true worth of the feast. We are not to come here complacently, or lightheartedly, or with outlandish clothes, but with deep searchings of heart and great appreciation of the wondrous Lord and Saviour, who is present in the midst.

May God help us so to come.

> According to Thy gracious word,
>   In meek humility,
> This will I do, my dying Lord;
>   I will remember Thee.
>
> Thy body, broken for my sake,
>   My bread from Heaven shall be;
> Thy blood my peace, this cup I take,
>   And thus remember Thee.
>
> When to the cross I turn my eyes,
>   And rest on Calvary,
> O Lamb of God, my sacrifice,
>   I must remember Thee!

JAMES MONTGOMERY

30

THE PROCLAMATION IN THE SUPPER

> Ye do shew [proclaim] the Lord's death (1 Corinthians 11:26).

The Lord's Supper is central to the Christian faith. It is very close to the spiritual affections of believers, and greatly treasured by those who know its value. It is one of the two ordinances which the Lord intended for the Church during His absence.

The first is baptism, which is an individual responsibility—a once-for-all act. The New Testament never contemplates an unbaptized believer. It is good to be a believer, but it is better to be a baptized believer.

The second ordinance is the Lord's Supper, and this is a corporate act, which should be observed with constant regularity. The remembrance feast must not be relegated to a secondary or inconspicuous place in the life of the assembly, much less set aside completely.

In this feast, believers look backward to the cross and remember the Lord's sufferings in their room and stead. They look upward to Heaven and remember that the Lord is risen, and that He is meat and drink for the sustenance of their present life in Him. They look forward and remember that He is coming again to receive them unto Himself.

The observance of this feast is something which the Lord has commanded us to keep: "This do!" Rarely did the Lord ask His people to do anything by way of commandment, but this He did, for very important purposes. His wisdom is clearly seen in such an assignment. We should of course, obey without the injunction, and without perceiving such wisdom. Ours is not to question the Lord's commands, but to trust and obey.

But then, the Lord does not treat us as infants, to be commanded without understanding. Rather does He treat us as adults with whom He shares His sovereign counsels, and to whom He explains His ways so that believers may more wholeheartedly cooperate with Him in carrying out His instructions.

The Historical Institution

This institution is given us in Matthew 26, Mark 14, and Luke 22. The prime emphasis is to remember Him in His death. Had it been left to His people to choose a memorial, some might have chosen a mighty miracle, a favorite parable, a song, a notable discourse. But no! The emphasis is placed by our Lord upon His death, on the offering up of Himself unto death on our behalf. The Lord thus imprinted His sacrificial death as central to the whole system of divine truth. This was the wisdom of God, for we, alas, are prone to forget that very thing.

In the course of church history there have been dark ages, days of spiritual declension, when our Lord's death was not the church's main emphasis. That sometimes shifted to a lust for temporal power, by means of which the church could raise up or depose kings of the realm, or to social reform, or to the making of creeds and credentials.

These things are never central if, indeed, some should ever have been present. That which is central is that which is unique—the substitutional and sacrificial death of the Lord Jesus. Happy the fellowship of believers who maintain that emphasis! The Lord did not come to earth primarily to relieve poverty by providing a bread ticket. Nor did He come primarily to instruct our ignorance. He came to deal with the fact and issues of sin, and make possible—through His sacrifice—the removal of our sins, reconciliation to God, restoration to His favor.

The course of church history has produced ministers, so-called, who deny the deity of Christ, His Godhood, His atoning death, and His bodily resurrection; who suggest that these ideas were invented by the Apostle Paul, that the Lord never claimed to be God, that His death was merely a noble example of self-sacrifice, that His body of flesh and bones never did come out of the tomb.

The institution of this feast confounds all these unholy breathings. It gives the lie to all such suppositions. His deity is evident in what He Himself said at the feast—in what His death would accomplish. Not even Moses, in his greatest flights of illumination, ever dared suppose that his death could remit sin. "This is My blood," said our Lord, "which is shed for many for the remission of sins" (Matthew 26:28). No other blood but His blood could avail to take away sins.

The Divine Insistence

Matthew seems to go out of his way to show that this memorial feast did not originate with the church, or with any apostle. He tells us that when the feast of the passover was nigh, Jewry's rulers said, when plotting His death, "Not on the feast day, lest there be an uproar among the people" (Matthew 26:5). But our Lord said, in effect, "on the feast day" (verse 2)—so that the type of the slain paschal lamb should have its fulfillment in Him on that God-appointed day. These things of God, you see, are never in the hands of men.

Then, again, the wisdom of our Lord in placing the emphasis upon His death is seen in what took place in the house of Simon the leper (Matthew 26:6-13). Simon's house would be shunned by the supposedly clean, but the undefilable Lord went to eat with Simon—for Him no infection could touch, and all diseases must obey. While in Simon's house, "There came unto Him a woman having an alabaster box of very precious ointment, and poured it on His head, as He sat at meat."

When one complained: "To what purpose is this waste?" the Lord defended the woman, saying, "She did it for My burial." She knew what the disciples were so slow to believe: that He must die. To emphasize again the primary importance of remembering His death, He shifts the emphasis from "the poor . . . for ye have the poor always with you; but Me ye have not always." Poverty is no barrier to being saved, or to entering Heaven—but sin is. Therefore, far more important than social reform and the relief of poverty is our Lord's death on the cross, without which no man can be saved and enter Heaven.

"Verily I say unto you," said the Lord Jesus, "Wheresoever this gospel shall be preached in the whole world, there shall also this, that this woman hath done, be told for a memorial of her"—that is, here was a woman with the right emphasis, as in the words of dying Jacob in Genesis 49:18, "I have waited for Thy salvation, O LORD." O wondrous, glorious cross! O wondrous death of Thine, Lord Jesus! Help us ever to remember it, and hold it in the primary place.

> I am not worthy: cold and bare
> The lodging of my soul;

How canst Thou deign to enter there?
Lord, speak, and make me whole.

I am not worthy; yet, my God,
How can I say Thee nay,
Thee, who didst give Thy flesh and blood
My ransom-price to pay?

O come, in this sweet hallowed hour,
Feed me with food divine;
And fill with all Thy love and power
This worthless heart of mine.

H. W. BAKER

31

THE PARTICIPATION IN THE SUPPER

Take, eat. . . . Drink ye all of it (Matthew 26:26-27).

We read of the institution of the Lord's feast in the Gospels, the celebration of it in the Acts of the Apostles, and the exposition of it in the Epistle to the Corinthians. In the institution of it, we read how the Lord first took bread, blessed it, and broke it (Matthew 26:26).

The First Mention

One of the most important principles of interpretation is the law of first mention. The first mention of bread and wine in Scripture is in Genesis 14:18: "Melchizedek king of Salem brought forth bread and wine: and he was the priest of the most high God." Melchizedek is one of the most outstanding types of the Lord Jesus, and here he meets Abraham with bread and wine. Abraham had been in battle, and he was worn and weary with the struggle. But through Melchizedek he is refreshed with bread and wine.

In this, we see a picture of our Lord's tender compassion for His people's needs. With Godlike bounty He presents every supply which wasted strength, sinking spirit, and failing heart require. The fight of faith is fierce; the journey of life often seems long. But at every step a banquet house is open, and food and drink are spread. Thus here in His feast there is the spiritual food of His own body given, His own blood shed. Our true Melchizedek invites us to draw near.

If we exclude this incident and look for the mention of the first making of bread, then we would find that in Genesis 18:3-6, where Abraham, visited by the Lord in some human form and with two attendants, thus addresses the central figure of the three: "My Lord . . . pass not away from thy servant . . . And I will fetch a morsel of bread. . . . And Abraham hastened into the tent unto Sarah, and said, Make ready quickly three measures of fine meal, knead it, and make cakes upon the hearth."

The fine meal is the same as that spoken of in the meat offering of Leviticus 2. This fine meal speaks of our Lord's impeccable character. There are no lumps in that holy character. He comes forth in all the beauty of sinless manhood.

But fine meal, too, is only formed by the crushing of the grain when the grinding mill reduces it to powder. The meal then is kneaded, and this speaks of the persecutions of men—their poundings of our Lord's holy body. He is the bruised God-Man, broken to make us whole. The kneaded bread was then baked "upon the hearth" of fire, which speaks of our Lord's bearing the awful wrath of divine justice. Thus we see in picture how our Lord became "the living bread" for our souls.

The Believer's Participation

In the institution of this feast, our Lord did four simple things with the bread. He took it, blessed it, broke it, and then gave it to His disciples. In doing so He said, "Take, eat; this is My body. And He took the cup, and gave thanks, and gave it to them, saying, Drink ye all of it."

The point to note is the believer's participation in this. He was involved. He was to partake both of the bread and of the wine, and to consume the elements. There is something more in this than simple reflection and remembrance of the historical event of the Lord's death. The feast was the token of the new testament. The beneficiaries of a testament only receive the inheritance after the testator's death. All the benefits of the Saviour's promises thus are now available to believers because Christ has died.

There is a beautiful picture given us in Luke of the believer's participation in the feast. The disciples said, when considering the passover, "Where wilt Thou that we prepare?" And the Lord Jesus said unto them, "Behold, when ye are entered into the city, there shall a man meet you, bearing a pitcher of water; follow him into the house where he entereth in. And ye shall say unto the goodman of the house, The Master saith unto thee, Where is the guestchamber, where I shall eat the passover with My disciples?" (Luke 22:9-11)

Jerusalem was a hostile city—red already with the blood of the prophets. The heart of the rulers was filled with hatred. They could not pity; they would not spare. "Come," said they, "let us kill him" (Matthew 21:38). Jesus' emblems had no charm for them. The altogether lovely One was never lovely in their eyes. The all-precious was counted vile. God's grandest gift was scorned.

But here, amidst the world's hostility, was one man who would prepare a place for the Lord in his home. The place was the best he had—a large upper room furnished and prepared (Mark 14:15). So it came to be that in this man's home the Lord, after beginning the passover feast, moved it into His own remembrance feast as a memorial of His approaching death—fulfillment in Himself of the slain paschal lamb of Jewish history.

Thus are we to partake. The best place in our heart's affections must be reserved for Him. We must come with hearts made ready. Let us remember that we live in a hostile world—a world full of enmity and hatred toward God's beloved Son. In the world lies sin's intense malignity. It is a cage of every foul bird—the nesting place for every impurity. We must loathe that world which slew our Lord and pierced His heart. Away with that which spared not Christ our Lord!

Nothing will help believers keep pure and wholesome more than the constant partaking of this remembrance feast. It warms the freezing air of this world. It will help you climb adversity's hill. It will enable you to struggle with resisting tides. It will revive and invigorate you each time you partake with a true heart. In these days, when the faith of many is found in soft attire, and there is much loitering in slothful ease, oh, let us be like this man in Jerusalem, ready with the best he has for the entertainment of the Lord—a joyful participant in this spread feast of love!

> O blessed, living Lord,
> Engage our hearts with Thee,
> And strike within the answering chord
> To love so rich and free!
>
> To know Thy loving heart!
> To cleave to Thy blest side!
> To gaze upon Thee where Thou art,
> And in Thy love abide!
>
> Be this our one desire,
> Thyself our object here,
> The goal to which our hearts aspire—
> To meet Thee in the air.
>
> JAMES BOYD

32

SOLOMON'S POINTERS TO CHRIST

> And Solomon offered a sacrifice of peace offerings, which he offered unto the LORD, two and twenty thousand oxen, and an hundred and twenty thousand sheep (1 Kings 8:63).

The greatness of the Person of the Lord Jesus is foreshadowed in Solomon. It is seen in his kingdom, his possessions, in his unique sonship. Solomon takes up a lot of space in Scripture, and this is indicative of his importance as a figure of Christ.

A Pointer to Our Lord's Death

The coronation of Solomon was celebrated with burnt offerings, which included a thousand rams, and a thousand lambs, with their drink offerings, and sacrifices in abundance (1 Chronicles 29:21). The magnifical temple built by Solomon was dedicated with peace offerings, which included "two and twenty thousand oxen, and an hundred and twenty thousand sheep." That meant death! Death! Death! All the time. This, together with millions of these sacrifices through the centuries, set forth something of the immensity of the sacrifice which was to be made by the Son of God. Yet these were but symbols, and symbols are but shadows of the real.

Moreover, the whole multitude of these sacrifices could not in themselves effect man's redemption. They were no more than emblems or pointers to the great sacrifice to come. They could not of themselves reach an end. It was necessary, therefore, that there be a constant repetition of them—today, tomorrow, and on through successive years and centuries of time. Neither could they deal with man's defiled conscience nor cleanse his heart from the guilt of sin. They "could not make him that did the service perfect, as pertaining to the conscience" (Hebrews 9:9).

Such sacrifices were external and ceremonial only; figurative and symbolical only. But the immensity of such sacrifices as offered by Solomon were pointers to the greatness of our Lord's death. His one offering on the cross accomplished what millions of these Jewish sacrifices could never do. "So Christ was once offered to bear the sins of many" (Hebrews 9:28). "We are sanctified through the offering of the body of Jesus Christ once for all" (Hebrews 10:10). "For by one offering He hath perfected for ever them that are sanctified" (Hebrews 10:14).

Why could not these thousands of offerings do that? Because there was present in our Lord's offering something not present in these animal offerings—a holy, spotless perfection. True, as far as priests could judge, those sacrifices had to be without blemish. But if you could have seen within the bloodstream, it would have been found that they belonged to a fallen creation. Their blood was by no means precious—that is, of rare worth—nor could their shed blood represent any love for the poor offerer.

Furthermore, our Lord's sacrifice was something greater than time. The doctrinal Epistles of Paul do not mention the physical sufferings which the historical records of the Gospels do. Why? Because there was something greater in the cross than what men did to Him. The evil of men was manifest in their crucifying Him, but beyond this was "the determinate counsel and foreknowledge of God" (Acts 2:23). The death of the Lord Jesus was no mere accident, nor was it simply His mistreatment by men. It was God's plan for human redemption. But, oh, how infinite was that cross! How vast that death!

A Pointer to the Lord's Resurrection

Solomon came to the throne when all his enemies had been conquered. He had no battles to fight. In his reign no enemy dare rise up against him. He was ruler over all with universal sway. How mighty was Solomon's name! In this he was a pointer to our Lord in resurrection life. Thus we catch a glimpse of our Lord, who rose from the dead to inherit all authority. In the days of His resurrection, while He was still lingering on earth, no enemy dare approach Him. All hell had been subdued and conquered.

In that resurrection there was a new relationship. In ancient times God said again and again to Solomon: "Solomon, My son"; not as to David: "David, My servant." So we hear God speak of the Lord Jesus in His resurrection life: "Thou art My Son, this day have I begotten Thee" (Acts 13:33).

There was also a new freedom. When Solomon came to the throne, he was free to move through his vast domain. So with our Lord in resurrection. He was no longer limited by a body of flesh. He breathed the air of resurrection liberty.

Again, there was a new realm of things. Solomon's reign was different. He was raised up to a new order of things. Listen to his prayer at the dedication of the Temple! What an intercessor! What a royal man of prayer! Does not this point to John 17, where the Lord takes up His mediatorial office on behalf of His people, and leaves us a record of magnificent intercession? How reviving to one's faith it is to hear it!

A Pointer to Our Lord's Exaltation

"And the LORD magnified Solomon exceedingly in the sight of all Israel, and bestowed upon him such royal majesty as had not been on any king before him in Israel" (1 Chronicles 29:25). He was set on a throne named "the throne of the LORD" (1 Chronicles 29:23). What a king

God made him! He was God's king. Righteousness charac-
terized his throne. His kingdom was first one of righteousness, then of peace—words which are full of weight. They
seat us on some height, as it were, to view in picture our
Lord's exaltation and His universal kingdom.

What is His Person—what His work—but the glory of
righteousness? His throne which is in Heaven, and which is
to be manifested here on earth in the millennium, is a throne
to dispense righteousness. Every statute, decree, ordinance,
precept, reward, and penalty is a sunbeam of righteousness.

And peace! Only in Christ and within the walls of
His kingdom, is there peace. Here, within these walls, there
is one song of perfect peace. And, thank God, the King of
righteousness and peace still calls men to His standard!

> Great God of wonders! all Thy ways
>   Are matchless, Godlike, and divine;
> But the bright glories of Thy grace
>   Above Thine other wonders shine.
> Who is a pardoning God like Thee?
> Or who has grace so rich and free?
>
> In wonder lost, with trembling joy,
>   We take the pardon of our God:
> Pardon for crimes of deepest dye,
>   A pardon bought with Jesus' blood.
> Who is a pardoning God like Thee?
> Or who has grace so rich and free?
>
> SAMUEL DAVIES

33

A NEW BEGINNING

This month shall be unto you the beginning of months (Exodus 12:2).

There is a distinct change here in the calendar. The new year was moved from autumn to spring, the time God redeemed Israel out of the bondage of Egypt. God made that physical redemption a wondrous picture of the spiritual redemption which we have in Christ Jesus our Lord. There was something tremendous in Israel's salvation.

It demonstrated Heaven's superiority over the whole organized empire of evil. It set forth God's purpose and intention to gather out of the nations a people for His name. All that pharaoh represented was drained to the last drop of its vitality and was laid in death. The exceeding greatness of God's power was toward His chosen people. God registered that day as a red-letter day—a day much to be remembered. So began a new year.

A New Beginning in Redemption

Until redemption was effected, Israel was under dominion of a foreign power—a mighty tyrant. The people were held in bondage, were made to do slavish tasks, were whipped by cruel taskmasters, and were driven to distraction. But God Himself saved them by a method of His own devising, and through it demonstrated the greatness of His power.

It began with a sacrifice of blood (Exodus 12:5-7). The blood of a lamb had not only to be shed, but had to be used by those who were to be saved by sprinkling it on the lintels and doorposts of their homes. Sheltering under the sprinkled blood, they were given God's guarantee of security when He would pass over Egypt in judgment. God said, "When I see the blood, I will pass over you" (Exodus 12:13). Their redemption, therefore, was founded on the shed blood of a substitutionary sacrifice.

They then fed on the roasted lamb (12:8). This was to give them strength for their coming journey. The sacrifice was to be "roast with fire"—a clear emblem of Christ suffering the wrath of God. God's hatred of sin must be shown: His majesty maintained, His truth preserved. His people, then, by feeding on the lamb, were to derive vigor and strength for their new journey of life.

Further, all leaven had to be purged out of their homes (12:15)—representing the putting away of all evil. "Purge out therefore the old leaven," said Paul in 1 Corinthians 5:7, as he took his figure from ancient Israel's command to sweep their homes of that which spoke of destructive evil.

Finally, they were to pass through the Red Sea: type of a new and living way—through death to life. It was a way that no man could make. It meant escape into life: a going down into the place of death to rise on ground of resurrection to live a new life.

A New Life Under Divine Government

The redeemed of the Lord were to have no earthly king. "This month shall be unto you the beginning of months." Why? "Because I redeemed you." Why did God redeem Israel? Not that they were to go on living as they once did. They were now to be under divine government—governed by the God of Heaven. In Egypt they had been a loose company, disorganized and scattered. Now they were molded into one people with the Lord Himself as their Head, their Teacher, their Defender.

They were fed with heavenly manna. Their new life began in a wilderness to teach them that this world could not supply any need. They were thus made utterly dependent upon God for the provision to maintain their new life—the manna which God sent from heaven picturing the coming Christ as "the living bread which came down from heaven" (John 6:51).

They were governed by heavenly principles. For four hundred years they had been slaves in Egypt, mixing with heathen, forced into compromises. Redemption separated them from all that! The Word of the living God was now to be the rule of their behavior.

They were instructed in heavenly worship. Life for them was now centered in the Tabernacle—a pattern of God's house in the heavens. Within the Tabernacle was a symbolic manifestation of God's holy presence in the Shekinah glory within the holiest of all. They were taught how to approach God through sacrifice, which prefigured Christ, and thus to be accepted of God in their worship.

They were assisted in heavenly guidance. The Lord went before them by a pillar of cloud by day and a pillar of fire by night. The wilderness was a trackless waste. They could not find their own paths. But the Lord was their Guide, their File Leader, and so forward they moved each day.

They were equipped with heavenly power. It was by this alone they were able to endure the trials of the journey and overcome all their enemies. So long as Moses held up hands in prayer, the Lord's people were kept safe from the assaults of Amalek. The Lord was a banner over them. They won through, not by the skill of their own fighting, but by the preserving power of God.

A New Destiny Through Divine Help

A new generation crossed the Jordan into the Promised Land. In typical teaching it meant a deeper identification with the death of Christ, a burial of selfism which had so plagued them in the wilderness. As they moved on to possess their possessions given them of God, there are three things to note.

First, the Lordship of Christ. He was represented in the appearance of "a man over against" Joshua, and He said, "As captain of the host of the LORD am I now come" (Joshua 5:13-14). He had come to take over.

Secondly, they ceased feeding on manna—that which came down from heaven and represented Christ in His life on earth. They now fed upon "the old corn of the land": that which grew upward out from the earth, and represented Christ in His resurrection and exaltation.

Thirdly, they were protected by a drawn sword. "There stood a man over against him with his sword drawn in his hand" (Joshua 5:13). There would be battle—warfare. But they were to be led forth in triumph by the Lord, and were to be protected by His defense of them. Through Him, they were to possess their possessions given them of God.

> Oh, teach us more of Thy blest ways,
>   Thou holy Lamb of God!
> And fix and root us in Thy grace,
>   As those redeemed by blood!
>
> For this, oh may we freely count
>   Whate'er we have but loss,
> The dearest object of our love,
>   Compared with Thee, but dross.
>
> Engrave this deeply on our hearts
>   With an eternal pen,
> That we may, in some small degree,
>   Return Thy love again.
>
> JAMES HUTTON

34

THREE PRECIOUSNESSES

The trial of your faith, being much more precious than of gold that perisheth (1 Peter 1:7).

Ye were . . . redeemed . . . with the precious blood of Christ (1 Peter 1:18-19).

He is precious (1 Peter 2:7).

Precious faith (2 Peter 1:1).

Persecution broke out after the martyrdom of Stephen. The world was mad in its hate as it has ever been. Believers were trodden as the mire beneath ungodly feet, and those who escaped death were scattered abroad. In his Epistles, Peter writes to the dispersed, and one of the words he uses over and over again is the word "precious."

Precious Faith

In 1 Peter 1:7 he mentions the trial of faith as being precious, and in 2 Peter 1:1 he says that faith itself is precious. Man's frown and persecution's threat give deadly wounds. We read in Bible history of many a tyrant's wrath, of the burning fiery furnace, of the den of raging lions, of stonings and imprisonments. The way to Heaven is often in the face of murderous batteries.

But faith can overcome! Multitudes upon multitudes with robes of white and palms of victory and songs of endless praise follow the Lamb whithersoever He goes. They do

124

not fear what man can do unto them.

Faith untried, unproved, is faith uncertain. The quality of the metal is ascertained by what it can do and bear. The courage of the soldier is evidenced only in the field of battle. The depth of the root of a tree is shown only by its resistance to a hurricane. Rock is solid only if it stands against all the surges of a raging sea. A foundation is strong only when it remains unshaken by batteries.

Trials do more than test the strength of faith. They consolidate and invigorate it. Its sinews become more firm. Those to whom faith has been given are not to count it strange that they have to swim against the tide. The trial is precious. It makes faith exceedingly precious. We are "to count it all joy when [we] fall into divers temptations."

Precious Blood

"Ye were not redeemed with corruptible things, as silver and gold . . . But with the precious blood of Christ" (1 Peter 1:18-19). His blood was not the polluted blood of a man of Adam's race. Our Lord did not come into the world by a man of fallen Adam's race, but the body prepared for Him was "conceived by the Holy Ghost."

Blood is the symbol of life. "The life of the flesh is in the blood" (Leviticus 17:11). The life of the eternal God was in the blood of the Lord Jesus as the Son of man. That is what made His blood precious. That life of His was offered for our redemption. The shedding of His blood was the pouring out of His blood as a sacrifice for sins. His cross was the theater of redeeming suffering—the atonement for the soul of man. We gaze with open eye upon His bloodstained cross, and know by divine certainty that He "purged our sins" (Hebrews 1:3).

We may there wash every stain away. The blood of Christ does that! We must remember that in His body—a truly human body—Deity was also present with His Manhood. He is the Mighty God. His blood is the blood of God (Acts 20:28). If it were less, it could effect no redemption. This is the marrow of the gospel. Jesus is God. He brings to the cross blood that is essentially divine. It is precious blood, and it is enough!

Also, His blood keeps on cleansing (1 John 1:7). This continued efficacy is not repetition of the sacrifice. Our Lord was "once offered"—the offering of His body was "once for all"—and He offered the one sacrifice "for ever." Calvary could never be repeated; never again could sacrifice be made for sins. That sacrificial blood has permanent value. It keeps on cleansing forever, not intermittently—not perhaps today but not tomorrow. That blood dealt with sins once and for all and forever.

Precious Lord

"He is precious" (1 Peter 2:7). This is spoken in the context where we are told that He is so as the chief cornerstone of God's spiritual house. Solomon came to the throne of Israel for the supreme purpose of building the Temple. Upon the completion of it, God's glory filled the whole. It was the embodiment of the glory of God. The stones that Solomon used for the building were cut out of a deep quarry, and were shaped, chiseled, and polished to a divine pattern. Each had its God-appointed place, and all fitted perfectly together.

Thus is it in God's spiritual house. The Lord Jesus builds with living stones—men and women made alive to God by the new birth. He is the chief Cornerstone—joining Jew and Gentile, bond and free, male and female, circumcision and uncircumcision, Scythian and barbarian. To all who are part of that spiritual house of His, "He is precious." They are what they are, and where they are, through His great sacrifice on the cross.

The Lord Jesus is the truest treasure man can ever gain. He is the sweetest cordial which the lips of faith can drink. He is Heaven's "sweet savor." There is none like our Lord—the Altogether-Lovely One! All peace and joy, all happiness and holiness are in Him, and in Him alone. "He is precious." May we ever prize Him so.

> Fairest Lord Jesus! Ruler of all nature!
>   O Thou, of God and man, the Son!
> Thee will I cherish, Thee will I honor,
>   Thou my soul's glory, joy, and crown!
>
> Fair is the sunshine, fairer still the moonlight,
>   And all the twinkling starry host;
> Jesus shines brighter, Jesus shines purer
>   Than all the angels Heaven can boast!
>
> All fairest beauty, heavenly and earthly,
>   Wondrously, Jesus, is found in Thee;
> None can be nearer, fairer, or dearer,
>   Than Thou my Saviour, art to me.

CRUSADERS' HYMN

35

SABBATH REST OF SOUL

There remaineth therefore a rest to the people of God
(Hebrews 4:9).

God's Creation Rest

Concerning the work of creation, we read that God ended the works which He had made in six days, and "rested on the seventh day from all His work which He had made" (Genesis 2:2). Why God should take six days to complete the work of creation belongs to His own chosen ways of wisdom and love. There is certainly much that is symbolic both in the order in which things were created and in the number of days taken to create them.

The seventh day, God's day of rest, was man's first full day of life, since he was made on the sixth day. The day of rest was instituted with man, and stands as the firstborn law and blessing. There are many intimations that this day of rest was observed long before the Sabbath of Judaistic law. Antediluvian times observed it. It told of God's rest when worlds were made.

But the Sabbath was instituted from the beginning because man needed it. Man's body is a wondrous fabric and was made for toil. But toil brings weariness and strain. Rest must repair it and renew its vigor. Rest must bring oil to the wheels to make it run smoothly and without a breakdown. Incessant labor brings dullness and ultimate collapse. In human history tyrants have arisen who have driven men to work seven days, and in so doing have broken their health and strength.

Israel's Sabbath Rest

When God brought Israel out of Egypt, He separated that nation from all other nations and fenced them round with the Law given from Mount Sinai. The majesty and sovereignty of God was manifested on the mount amidst rolling thunder and flashing lightning. God made Himself known there as the moral Ruler of the universe. Central to that moral Law was the sabbath day of rest. Even before the Law was given on Mount Sinai, the Sabbath of rest was observed (Exodus 16:23).

On the Sabbath no manna fell from heaven, and the Israelites were forbidden to seek it. "To morrow is the rest of the holy sabbath unto the LORD." But in Exodus 20 God's own finger wrote on tables of stone what had been written on the tables of man's heart in creation. The Sabbath belongs to creation's law, and was reiterated and reemphasized at the beginning of Israel's history as a nation. Through the centuries of time the prophets of Israel inveighed against any breach of the rest of the holy Sabbath.

The Believer's Redemptive Rest

The Lord Jesus spoke of Himself as "the Lord of the sabbath," and said that "the sabbath was made for man." That is a word which looks backward to tell us that there has always been a day of rest, for man always had need of such. It is also a word which looks forward to the future, and declares man will always have need of a rest day.

Then came Calvary's cross, and the same Scriptures of truth which tell us of creation ended tell us now of redemption completed. Thus there are really only two completed works—creation and redemption. Israel's Sabbath of rest was but a reiteration and reemphasis of what had been from the beginning and was a type of the second rest which was to come in Christ.

With the coming of the Saviour, all things in Judaism came to an end. Its rites and ceremonies died as autumn leaves from a tree. But moral law is reemphasized in the New Testament—being a natural expression of the life of God given to those who believe in the Lord Jesus. The day of rest did not cease but the Judaistic form of this day, which was but a symbol, was done away. There was, therefore, an end to the Jewish Sabbath for believers. It did not apply to them.

Man still needs the day of rest given in his creation. Both body and mind need it; but, far more important, such a day is for the refreshing of our spirits. It is a day when we must shut out the world and give ourselves to waiting upon God to offer worship, praise, and thanksgiving.

The believer's sabbath rest is found, not in a certain day, but in the Person of the Lord Himself. He is our rest. God rests in Him. Each attribute of the divine nature finds repose in His blessed Person and work. Justice has claims, but the Lord Jesus pays all. Truth has claims, but the Lord Jesus fulfills every word. Holiness has claims, but the Lord Jesus more than satisfies. Mercy and love have claims, but the Lord Jesus gives them their fullest exercise. The Lord

Jesus is God's Sabbath throughout Heaven.

Trusting souls on earth rest in Him. The duties and paths of ritualistic observance brought no rest to Israel. None of such observances can remove guilt or cleanse from sins. Under such a load how weary and languid men were! But in the Lord Jesus weary sinners have found rest for their souls. He Himself is our sabbath rest of soul.

This is why Heaven is spoken of as a place of rest. It is so because the Lord Jesus is there. Heaven *is* Heaven because there is an eternal rest in the presence of the Lord.

To nurture the rest of the whole man, believers have set aside, from the beginning of the church age, our Lord's resurrection day as a day of rest—a memorial to His completed work of redemption. This day has Old Testament sanction, as for instance in the feast of first fruits, when one sheaf only was gathered and taken into the Temple and waved before the Lord. This was done, not on the seventh, but the eighth day, our Sunday, resurrection day. This might remind us of creation's rest day, when God's seventh day was man's first day. Let not Satan rob us of this. Let us not make it a common day. Let nothing disfigure it. Let us keep it as a holy day, and drive the devil back by making it a day of worship, praise, adoration, and meditation upon holy things.

> Jesus, before Thy face we fall—
> Our Lord, our life, our hope, our all!
> For we have nowhere else to flee—
> No sanctuary, Lord, but Thee!
>
> In Thee we ev'ry glory view,
> Of safety, strength, and beauty, too:
> 'Tis all our rest and peace to see
> Our sanctuary, Lord, in Thee!
>
> Whatever foes or fears betide,
> In Thy blest presence we abide;
> And while we rest our souls in Thee,
> Thou wilt our sanctuary be.
>
> SAMUEL MEDLEY

36

THE LORD AND HIS FRIENDS

The LORD . . . will not suffer the destroyer to come in
unto your houses to smite you (Exodus 12:23).

Ye are My friends (John 15:14).

The whole purpose of our Lord's redeeming sacrifice
is to have those with Him who shall be His companions
forever. The fellowship with Him in the remembrance feast
is a beautiful expression of that companionship.

Before the Lord instituted the feast, Judas had gone
out. He had proved to be a traitor, not a friend. When Judas
went out, a whole nation went out with him, for he was
a representation of the whole—a nation which had rejected
Jesus as the Christ, the Son of the living God, and which
was now rejected by Him. With Judas gone, the Lord was
left with His true companions.

The Lord's Supper is one of the great features of tran-
sition from Israel of the old covenant to the Church of the
new. What the passover feast was intended to mean to
Israel is made real in the Lord's remembrance feast to His
Church.

The Judgment Upon Evil

In the night the passover was instituted, the Lord was
to bring judgment upon Egypt and its gods. The first of
God's commandments is: "Thou shalt have no other gods
before Me." But the Egyptians had made gods out of frogs
and those many other things brought out in the plagues.

131

God's judgment was not only against Egypt but against the gods of Egypt. There was to be no compromise for His people Israel with such evil. All blessedness was in God, the living God, and this meant separation from all that was represented by Egypt.

After smiting the gods of Egypt, the judgment of God was to smite the firstborn. The firstborn represented the whole family, including parents. The firstborn also embodied the principle that that which is first is natural (1 Corinthians 15:46). In God's scheme of things the natural is set aside. Natural birth has transmitted to all men a corrupt nature, and it has brought them into a world of sin.

It is important to remember that, as the Lord's people through spiritual birth, believers have been transported into a new world of grace. There must be no compromise with sin and that which is false. This is the first principle of gathering unto the Lord. God's judgment upon that which is the fruit of a corrupt natural life thus makes way for that which is spoken in 1 Corinthians 15:46: "afterward that which is spiritual"—which is "the church of the firstborn" or "first-born ones" (Hebrews 12:23).

The Importance of the Threshold

In the passover, the blood of the paschal lamb was gathered in a basin and put on the threshold. From that basin the lintel and the side posts were struck with blood. None were to cross that threshold. "None of you shall go out at the door of his house until the morning" (Exodus 12:22). The threshold was a most sacred place. It divided between what was in, and what was outside, the house— friends or enemies of the Lord. If any Israelite went out of his house, he would be in the camp of the enemy and thus would be smitten in judgment. The sprinkled blood on the door insured their safety so long as they abode under its protective covering.

Before the Lord moved into His remembrance feast, Judas had already crossed the threshold into the camp of the enemy. He was not, as it were, under the sprinkling of the blood. The blood so despised and profaned by him brought upon him a tremendous woe. He scorned the grand reality. The doorposts of his heart were without blood, and thus there was no protection for him against the messenger of death. Betrayal brought him to that!

The blood-besprinkled threshold of old marked the division. When God saw the blood, He said to the destroying angel, if such there was: "Don't go in there. They are My friends." The friends were those within the shelter of the blood. God's own word was: "When I see the blood, I will pass over you" (Exodus 12:13). Said Moses: "When He seeth the blood . . . the LORD will pass over the door, and will not suffer the destroyer to come in unto your houses to smite you" (Exodus 12:23). The matter of judgment was settled on the threshold—judgment outside; security inside.

The Night of Betrothal

The passover feast was really a betrothal ceremony. "I took them by the hand to bring them out of the land of Egypt . . . I was an husband unto them, saith the LORD" (Jeremiah 31:32). That was the passover night when God made a covenant with Israel. It was a blood covenant—a blood relationship. It was because of the breach of this betrothal covenant by Israel that God called their departure to serve other gods "whoredom," "fornication," and "adultery."

"My covenant they brake" (Jeremiah 31:32). That is why Israel was set aside. They trampled down the blood covenant—and the blood was precious since it typified Christ's blood. Blood could flow only from an expiring victim. It spoke of death as the desert of sin. But it was also the witness to redemption—God's method of accomplishing redemption—and thus it was linked to expiating grace. All this Israel despised in her breach of her betrothal to the living God.

So Jesus came and gathered a new society of friends with Himself as the Mediator of a better covenant, established upon better promises (Hebrews 8:6). So the night of the institution of the Lord's Supper was not only the night of His betrayal by Judas, but of His betrothal to His Church. He betrothed the Church to Himself in a covenant of blood— His blood. "This is the new covenant in My blood"—and by that precious shed blood He has secured His believing people to Himself forever.

What a union!—a union which cements our hearts to the Lord Jesus, and the Lord Jesus to us. In this present age believers are betrothed to Him by covenant blood. Soon, soon now, the day of marital union will arrive—"Behold, the bridegroom cometh," and so, "Let us be glad and rejoice, and give honour to Him: for the marriage of the Lamb is come, and His wife hath made herself ready" (Revelation 19:7).

> Oh, Christ! He is the fountain,
>   The deep, sweet well of love!
> The streams on earth I've tasted
>   More deep I'll drink above:
> There, to an ocean fullness
>   His mercy doth expand,
> And glory, glory dwelleth
>   In Immanuel's land.
>
> The bride eyes not her garment,
>   But her dear Bridegroom's face:
> I will not gaze at glory,
>   But on my King of Grace—
> Not at the crown He giveth,
>   But on His pierced hand:
> The Lamb is all the glory
>   Of Immanuel's land.

ANNE ROSS COUSIN

37

FEASTING UNTO ONGOING

> And thus shall ye eat it; with your loins girded, your
> shoes on your feet, and your staff in your hand; and ye
> shall eat it in haste: it is the LORD's passover (Exodus
> 12:11).

When we assemble for worship and remembrance meeting, we look for something to strengthen us for the coming days. The twelfth chapter of Exodus records the institution of the passover feast in Israel. Every fragment of that feast holds within its embrace spiritual principles which apply to our Lord's own remembrance feast. These ancient ceremonies are the pleasure ground of spiritual minds, and the way to ever-revealing views of Christ Jesus our Lord. The Old Testament is a boundless mine. The more we dig, the richer the treasure.

Israel's Ongoing

The passover feast had this cautionary word: "Thus shall ye eat it;" that is, not anyhow, not with a slothful spirit, not with indulgent ease, but with "loins girded . . . shoes on your feet . . . staff in your hand." They were to be ready for a forward movement toward the Lord's promised inheritance in Canaan.

Though their deliverance would be wholly of the Lord—and that by a new and living way through the place of death in the Red Sea trough—the journey would require putting forth every ounce of strength on their part. This strength was to be derived from feeding on the slain paschal lamb. Thus, before beginning the journey, they were to be partakers of the same

135

lamb whose sprinkled blood had sheltered and secured them on the night God passed over Egypt in judgment.

We read at one point that, after their deliverance and while journeying on, Moses said to his father-in-law, Hobab, "We are journeying unto the place of which the LORD said, I will give it you" (Numbers 10:29). They were a people on the march. Life now was to be an onward progress to the promised land. God the Lord was to go before them; they were to follow Him. He would lead and guide. Unless He does so none can find their paths—for this world is a barren waste.

Moses pressed on Hobab an invitation to join them, and he did so with the promise of good: "for the LORD hath spoken good concerning Israel." So Moses reasoned. But Hobab was not settled. His feelings fluctuated. He hesitated. He looked toward the attractions of an earlier scene, and to that he returned—never to enter the promised land. To go back, as Hobab did, is to clasp a shadow, to grasp a nettle, to lean on a broken reed.

When Moses stated the fact about the promised land, there was no uncertainty about it though it was some distance away. In guiding, God does not deceive. The promised land was a heavenly pledge. What a happy state it is to be "in the faith"! Faith has an eagle eye and will quicken the step. It can see through the mists and darkness of the present. It cannot settle for anything else than God's promised land.

The eating of the passover feast with such readiness meant a great urge in the Lord's people to move onward into what surely would be rest. There would be no more burdens to bear, no more enemies to fight. The watchword, therefore, was "Let us go on." Their new life in redemption called for that! The promised land urged them forward. The passover feast fortified them for the journey.

Our Lord's Ongoing

At the end of His upper room discourse, the Lord said something similar: "Arise, let us go hence" (John 14:31).

In that room the shadow of the cross had fallen upon the hearts of the disciples. But, said the Lord, "Let not your heart be troubled"—everything is going to be all right.

In Philippians 2:5-8 Paul shows us something of the Lord's journey from the heights of glory down to the shame of the cross. It was a going down—a laying aside of everything in order to accomplish something. He would brush everything aside for man's redemption. There was to be no delay. Nothing was to stand in the way. Love for us was the one pulse of His heart. He would come to purchase an eternal inheritance for us. That would be a gift worthy of God, who gave it; worthy of the blood the Son of God would shed to purchase it; worthy of the Holy Spirit who would call us to it.

So, also, when here on earth, the Lord set His face steadfastly toward the cross. There was no withholding, no loitering, no hanging back. When Peter tried to hold Him back, the Lord Jesus soundly rebuked him. In His sufferings and death alone could there be redemption. Then mark His firm step, His loins girt, shoes on His feet, staff in hand, as it were. There was no hesitation in His coming from Heaven to earth. Nor was there hesitation in His going to Calvary. He was journeying to a prearranged end—God's end.

The Believer's Ongoing

Believers are part of a marching host. Earth is not their rest. They live a stranger-life. They hold a pilgrim staff. They must march on. Their anchor must not be cast in sand. Their affections must not entwine around earthly stems. Their home and mansions are on high. A journey lies before them.

The note struck at the paschal feast reverberates also at the Lord's Supper. "Let us go on," wrote the apostle to the Hebrew Christians. There is a real link between Israel's paschal feast—the note struck at our Lord's remembrance feast—and the life to be lived by His redeemed ones. "I press toward the mark," said Paul (Philippians 3:14). The theme is one. In each case, all impediments are to be laid aside for an ongoing—a pursuit—a quest. The whole Bible is taken up with this. To make ongoing the best possible, absolute obedience is required. There is something in this feast—something timeless, something strengthening—which will help us to go on in a spiritual way.

There are difficulties in the way. There were difficulties in Israel's ongoing. There were such in the way for our Lord. There will be for us. Our foes are many, mighty, wily, restless. They lurk in every place, waiting to assault. The world, too, opposes with its snares, temptations, foul seductions, enticing lusts, siren smiles, terrible threats. But we are to go on. Nothing will better give us strength for the journey than the constant remembrance of the sacrifice of our Lord and our feeding upon Him.

> Come, Thou Fount of every blessing,
>   Tune my heart to sing Thy grace;
> Streams of mercy, never ceasing,
>   Call for songs of loudest praise.
> Teach me, Lord, some rapturous measure,
>   Meet for blood-bought hosts above;
> While I sing the countless treasure
>   Of my God's unchanging love.
>
> Jesus sought me when a stranger,
>   Wandering from the fold of God;
> He, to save my soul from danger,
>   Interposed His precious blood.
> Rescued thus from sin and danger,
>   Purchased by the Saviour's blood,
> May I walk on earth a stranger,
>   As a son and heir of God.

ROBERT ROBINSON

38

THE MEDIATOR OF THE NEW COVENANT

He is the mediator of the new testament (Hebrews
9:15).

The Lord by His sacrifice is able to purify the conscience
and cleanse the heart of man. These effects were not possible
under the old covenant. Therefore a new covenant was brought
in, but not until the old covenant had received all the honor
which its tremendous sanctions demanded. Death was its
demand for transgression, and this it received on behalf of us
all by one of the covenant-makers, the Son of God. This led
the Hebrew believers to have respect for what, naturally,
they hated most—the doctrine of a crucified Messiah.

The New Covenant

The efficacious sacrifice of the Lord Jesus and His
prevailing mediation needed a new covenant to suit them.
New wine could not be put into old bottles. Therefore, He
who offered the sacrifice and opened the way into the holiest
is by necessity the Mediator of the better covenant. The old
covenant, not being able to pacify conscience and cleanse
the heart of man, could not bring us into an eternal inheritance. But the eternal inheritance was what God had
promised to the father of believers, Abraham. Yet none could
possess it under the old covenant. This meant a further
necessity for a new covenant.

The new covenant really existed from the beginning—
for our Lord was slain, as it were, from before the foundation of the world, His sacrifice being already in the mind

of God. The covenant is based on the rock of God's unchangeable and eternal purpose. It must be clearly understood that this covenant, which is the believer's safeguard, is not a covenant made with sinful man. The covenant of works was made with man, and was instantly broken. Such a violated treaty can be no plea before God. Through violation we are heirs of wrath.

The new covenant is made between the Father and the Son on our behalf. The Lord Jesus stands before God as a second man in the place of the first man who had failed. God commits to His Son the terms of the covenant and the promises attached. The Father binds Himself to these terms and makes promises. Thus the Father, in His office as God, pledges Himself to those who shall be saved. His Son, in His office as Mediator, pledges, on our behalf, to fulfill the terms of the covenant, and so make us inheritors of the pledged promises.

God's terms are that man be cleansed from all sin and be clothed in all righteousness—thoroughly renewed and acceptable to God in every way. The Lord Jesus undertakes to present before God such a people, and will Himself be responsible for the full performance of the work. God promises to be their God; Christ promises that they shall be His people.

This covenant has the promise, then, of an eternal inheritance (Hebrews 9:15). This is what God promised Abraham and David. Our Lord's sacrifice was designed not only to take away the sins of new covenant believers but also those of true believers under the old covenant. Those believers of old, therefore, have not perished.

The new covenant was ratified by death (Hebrews 9:16-17). The ancient method of making covenants was to place a slain victim between two parties. The covenant was ratified over a dead body—meaning that any breach of it would issue in the death of the one who breached it. So the Lord Jesus has atoned for our sins by His death. In that death the old covenant is honored, but a new covenant is now established.

This everlasting covenant was confirmed to Moses (Hebrews 9:18-22). The idea of substitution was never absent from ancient God-given rites. You see that in the coats of skins given Adam and Eve, in Abraham's offering Isaac, in the ram's taking the place of Isaac, and so many more. The breach of the old covenant made with man teaches us that we are sinners condemned to death. The glory of the new covenant is that God accepts a Substitute, even His own beloved Son, who met all the demands of that broken covenant, and established believers in a new and better covenant.

The Efficacious Sacrifice

First, the sacrifice of our Lord cleanses heavenly things (Hebrews 9:23-24). These heavenly things are explained by the pattern—Israel's people, the earthly tabernacle, the vessels of ministry. All heavenly things needed to be meet for us, and we made meet for Heaven. Our Lord's sacrifice preserves from that which would defile. Our presence in Heaven would defile it except that the Lord Jesus appears in the presence of God for us. Thus when we follow Him into Heaven no dishonor is done. The Lord is there on God's behalf and on our behalf. Thus the sacrifice of Christ prepares Heaven for us, and prepares us for Heaven.

Secondly, the sacrifice of our Lord deals with the root of sin (Hebrews 9:25-26). In the old economy, the sacrifices of Jewry had to be repeated, and they could be repeated only if the land produced enough bullocks and goats. With our Lord, His sacrifice was so complete and efficacious that it would never have to be repeated. It was too excellent to be repeated. There were millions of bulls and goats but only one Son of God. He could die but once. The Jewish high priests came out of the earthly tabernacle each year looking for more bulls and goats, but Christ abides in the heavenly tabernacle forever, His object having been fully accomplished.

Thirdly, the sacrifice of our Lord prepares us for His return (Hebrews 9:27-28). When our Lord came "to bear the sins of many," He could be offered only once.

But the apostle warns these indolent Hebrew Christians of His reappearance, and that this reappearance will not be after the manner of the Jewish high priests who reappeared after being in the earthly tabernacle. They came out to offer new sacrifices. Our Lord's reappearance means the receiving of His saints and the destruction of His enemies. He is to appear without any sin offering—that is, not for the purpose of making sacrifice for sins again.

Before the throne of God above
  I have a strong, a perfect plea;
A great High Priest, whose name is Love,
  Who ever lives and pleads for me.

My name is graven on His hands,
  My name is written on His heart;
I know that while in Heav'n He stands
  No tongue can bid me thence depart.

Behold Him there! the risen Lamb!
  My perfect, spotless righteousness,
The great unchangeable I AM,
  The King of glory and of grace!

CHARITIE LEES BANCROFT

39

THE CONQUEST OF THE WORLD

Now is the judgment of this world (John 12:31).

The world in its material form is not in itself evil. There was neither disorder nor ugliness in it when God first made it. When the work of creation was completed, God pronounced it "very good." It was wonderfully adapted to be man's home. It was the garden of the Lord—an earthly paradise. The whole planet reflected the goodness of God. Fragrance and fruit charmed and refreshed man's senses. To live there, as man did in the primeval setting, and to converse with God was surely unalloyed delight. Man's heart was only love; his worship was pure praise of his Creator.

But in yielding to Satan, the first man yielded not only his heart to the prince of evil, but also the earth over which God had made him overseer. Satan, therefore, has been able to build upon the earth, using unregenerate man, a world system without reference to God. There are many parts to that system, each of which appeals to different persons, but all draw away worship and reverence from the living God.

The Appeal of the World

The world has been made most appealing to the natural man. Its secularized society appeals to each person according to his temperament. It has a religious appeal. A multitude of humanitarian religions, modeled after Cain's, reject the blood-sacrifice of Christ. Thus, while being religious, such devotees are under the curse, for, like Cain, they are "of that wicked one." This is manifest in their rejecting God's method of redemption. The world's religious systems are rooted in man's own works.

The world has an educational appeal. This offers a degree of learning in all natural sciences, but it will never teach God's truth, that truth written in the Scriptures—the only Book of truth in this untrue world. The educational system will even provide courses in the occult but not courses in the revealed truth of God.

The world has a commercial appeal. This inspires men to grab all they can of material possessions but to seek no sustenance for their souls. The whole emphasis is either on the body or the soul but none on the spirit.

The world has a political appeal. This is government without God. Since man's reason is totally in darkness, his affections unclean, and his will disobedient to God's will, the inevitable result is governmental chaos. He rules corruptly over sin-doomed earthly kingdoms where corruption abounds.

The world has a recreational appeal. This is an appeal to make people's lives full of fun and sport, filled with mirth and laughter to make men lovers of pleasure, worshipers of the god of this world, admirers of its vanity, indulgers of its flesh.

The world, then, is a great distraction. Satan sees to it that there is little time for hearing the Word of God, and makes that Word irksome to itching ears. It is a world full of idols, all of which speak vanity. It pretends to have what it does not possess. It offers what it cannot provide. Satan is very skillful to whisper that these things must have their proper place.

But his design in the whisper is to put the things of God out of every place. The world is a satanic system which draws the love of fallen man into foolish vanities, empty shows, golden maxims, defiling pleasures, lying principles, soul-beclouding literature, and makes an idol of all the wit and talent of the natural man. The world binds the souls of men to Satan's chariot.

The Overcoming of the World

"I have overcome the world." So said the Lord Jesus, and we must believe it. But how did He do that? He did it by living a godly life in the midst of a godless society. He never withdrew from the world of men. He did not shut Himself up in a monastery. He mixed with men. "Then drew near unto Him all the publicans and sinners for to hear Him" (Luke 15:1). He trod this earth in human nature and in human form, moving among men and sharing their toil.

In His life on earth our Lord used very little of this world's goods. He was not allured by its appeals. Thus He who alone could choose, chose for His birthplace a lowly manger in a cattle shed; for His family, a very poor one; and for His place of upbringing, Nazareth, a city infamous for crime. During His ministry He chose to have nowhere to lay His head. He overcame the world, not with money—that were vain. He used no finite store—that would fall short. He lived a perfect, sinless life. The world, therefore, had no appeal to Him. It failed to allure Him. He overcame it by a life of impeccable holiness. He alone fulfilled all righteousness—each righteous ordinance of God. The world had nothing in Him to which it could appeal. He overcame the world.

As the world could not allure Him, so also it could not frighten Him to deflect Him from the Father's will and purpose. Oh, the world would assault Him with the cruelest of torture. The world would prove a monster of unspeakable hatred—a world of evil men who would slay the Lord of glory and become inflicters of all His stripes. It would not spare Him. It would pierce His body and His heart, but it could never deflect Him from God's great purpose. He remained a quenchless flame until the redemption of fallen man was an accomplished fact.

> Take the world, but give me Jesus;
> All its joys are but a name;

But His love abideth ever,
　　Through eternal years the same.

　Chorus:
　O the height and depth of mercy!
　　O the length and breadth of love!
　O the fullness of redemption,
　　Pledge of endless life above!

Take the world, but give me Jesus;
　Sweetest comfort to my soul;
With my Saviour watching o'er me,
　I can sing though billows roll.

Take the world, but give me Jesus;
　In His cross my trust shall be;
Till, with clearer, brighter vision,
　Face to face my Lord I see.

FANNY J. CROSBY

40

THE CONQUEST OF THE DEVIL

　　Now shall the prince of this world be cast out (John 12:31).

In Revelation 5:5 the Apostle John was told not to weep because "the Lion of the tribe of Juda, the Root of David, hath prevailed to open the book, and to loose the seven seals thereof." And when John turned to see the Lion, he saw "a Lamb as it had been slain"—which means that the Lord Jesus had won a complete victory over "that old serpent, called the Devil, and Satan" (Revelation 12:9; 20:2); and He did so on the cross as the Lamb of God.

The world is full of sin, and only God's Word gives us the fact of how it entered. The devil, in the form of an enticing and seducing serpent, that is "a shining one," deceived our first parents and, by prevailing over them, changed their nature.

The moving cause of our being born in sin, and living in sin, is clear. It is the devil. He is a mighty, skillful, and malignant power. He is "the prince of this world" (John 12:31). His sway is worldwide. All men, by the derivation of their life from Adam, are born the slaves of Satan, to whom Adam had yielded himself, and soon they begin to do his evil works.

Nor can men free themselves. His fetters are strong. "Ye are of your father the devil, and the lusts of your father ye will do." So said our Lord in John 8:44. And that devil is "the god of this world" (2 Corinthians 4:4). He has attractive idols and decks them with great show. The world is full of them. Multitudes worship at their shrines. Because the devil is a spirit, he has access to the secret places of the human heart.

The first promise of God was that the promised Seed of the woman (Christ) would bruise Satan's head. As soon, therefore, as man was ruined, he who ruined him was also doomed to ruin. The devil's temporary success was to end in his own final defeat and despair. In the fullness of time the Saviour came. Our Lord went unto the death of the cross to meet this great enemy in his own stronghold. At that cross the Lord Jesus not only defeated Satan and stripped him of his power as a personal victory, but He did so on our behalf, so that we might share that victory.

The Natural View

To the natural eyes of men, the cross would not have appeared a victory for our Lord. It would have been impossible for any natural man to look at the cross and think of Jesus as a conqueror. He had been rejected by His own nation, betrayed by Judas, denied by Peter, deserted by His disciples, condemned by pagan Rome, seized by evil men, nailed to a cruel cross; then He bowed His head and died. It would surely have appeared that even Jesus was now held in Satan's prison of death, and that He would be detained there.

The conquest of Satan was costly to God's beloved Son. The first promise in Genesis 3:15 spoke of it—that the serpent would "bruise Thy heel," that is, the lower part of His being—His body. That became true when our Lord's "visage was so marred more than any man" (Isaiah 52:14). The detail of His sufferings is written largely in Psalm 22, and includes the awful words: "All My bones are out of joint" (verse 14). This was His bruising!

The battle was first joined when the Son of God came into the world as the Son of man. In the days of His ministry on earth, His authority over the powers of hell was manifest in His casting out of demons. There were evidences of the evil one's retreat from the Lord. In each of such cases the Lord Jesus was plundering the strong man's palace and was taking his goods.

The Divine View

The Bible insists that the Lord won a complete victory in the cross over all the powers of hell. The final battle was joined in the cross. The categorical statements of Colossians 2:15 and Hebrews 2:14 make this clear: "And having spoiled principalities and powers, He made a shew of them openly, triumphing over them in it [the cross]." "Forasmuch then as the children are partakers of flesh and blood, He also himself likewise took part of the same; that through death He might destroy him that had the power of death, that is, the devil."

The Lord disarmed Satan so that never again did he have a weapon to raise against the Son of God, which fact is manifest in our Lord's postresurrection days and in His ascension. The devil dare not approach Him.

In His dealing with Adam's race, the devil brought

the whole race under his power. Then, when the Son of God became Son of man, the strategy of Satan was to wait until the Lord was "crucified [in] weakness," and then to fling all the powers of hell at Him, hoping to overcome Him. But the Lord flung them off, "triumphing over them."

The end of the combat shows where victory is! Our Lord burst the doors of death, came forth from the dead, showed Himself alive, ascended in triumph to the throne of God, and is now proclaimed "the LORD mighty in battle" (Psalm 24:8).

The word "destroy" does not mean to annihilate. The Lord Jesus did not annihilate Satan. The word means "to render idle" or "ineffective." It also means "unproductive." The devil does indeed retain power over those who are his slaves, but he has been stripped of all power over the Lord Jesus and those who abide in Him.

> A mighty fortress is our God,
> A bulwark never failing;
> Our Helper He, amid the flood
> Of mortal ills prevailing.
> For still our ancient foe
> Doth seek to work us woe;
> His craft and power are great,
> And, armed with cruel hate,
> On earth is not his equal.
>
> Did we in our own strength confide
> Our striving would be losing;
> Were not the right Man on our side,
> The Man of God's own choosing.
> Dost ask who that may be?
> Christ Jesus, it is He;
> Lord Sabaoth His name,
> From age to age the same,
> And He must win the battle.

MARTIN LUTHER

41

THE CONQUEST OF THE FLESH

A body hast Thou prepared Me. . . . Then said I, Lo,
I come . . . to do Thy will, O God (Hebrews 10:5,7).

The flesh is nearer to us than either the devil or the world. It is part of us. There was no original evil in the body which God provided for the first man, Adam. True, it had a very lowly origin—"Dust thou art." It is almost as though God, foreknowing the fall of man, made him of dust to counter the pride that would rise in him through sin. In this body, then, we have a common parentage with worms, since both are created creatures. The fleshly body is no more than the dust beneath our feet—a shell of clay.

The Fall of Man

When God breathed into man's nostrils the breath of life, man became a living soul. That man had a God-given, created life. He was perfect in his innocence, and his body functioned perfectly as an instrument of that God-breathed life. The smile of his innocence met the smile of God. But he was merely a created creature, and a creature must obey. It is so with the angels in Heaven. On earth it must also be so with man. God must rule in His own universe.

Obedience, however, was to be no heavy burden. In a lovely garden where man was given to eat of all the trees, only one was forbidden. Only one command was issued: "In the day that thou eatest thereof thou shalt surely die" (Genesis 2:17).

So the tempter came. Innocent life is not spiritual life. To acquire spiritual life there must be voluntary choice, for piety untried is piety uncertain. With subtilty the snare is laid. Evil suggestion is presented. The one command is broken. Sin enters. Communion with God dies immediately. The spirit of man is dead to God. The mind, without the God-known spirit to enlighten, is plunged into blackness and darkness. The affections become unclean, the will disobedient. Instead of being theocentric—God-centered—the man becomes egocentric—self-centered, and that with a fallen self, a godless self.

Thus the fallen self makes the body of flesh "an instrument of unrighteousness" to do all manner of uncleanness. All the human race have come to be what Adam was, by the line of heredity from him.

Paul develops the thought that both the soul and the body of fallen man are "the flesh"—the flesh of the body now governed by a fleshly or carnal nature. Thus "in me (that is, in my flesh,) dwelleth no good thing" (Romans 7:18). The whole nature, ruled by a godless principle, is spoken of as "the flesh."

The appeal of this fallen man is simply this: live like an animal which has only soul and body! Let the whole thought of your human existence revolve around "What shall we eat? or, What shall we drink? or, Wherewithal shall we be clothed? [e.g., keep warm]" (Matthew 6:31) and fill it to the full with sexual satisfaction. That is animal life. God is not in such a life. We are all fleshly in the fleshliness of Adam. We are what he became. In him we receive that heritage of the curse. In him we enter this carnal existence and become clothed with this sensuous and fleshly life.

The Triumph of Christ

The Lord Jesus was given a body—not a body derived from man's activity, nevertheless a real body, specially formed for Him in the womb of Mary by the Holy Spirit. In that body the Lord Jesus kept the whole law of God. The body of His flesh was kept in absolute purity. "Holiness unto the Lord" is God's standard. "Ye shall be holy; for I am holy" (Leviticus 11:44). God can accept no inferior standard. As the Son of man our Lord walked on earth as on heavenly ground. Mark His every act. Hear His every word. All is holiness unto the Lord. No trial was spared Him. Hell's every snare was laid for Him. No circumstance failed to put forth its craftiest wiles. But He did no sin. He was undefiled and undefilable. He was perfect holiness.

But this holiness of His had to be wrought out for His people. It is this which led Him to Calvary's cross. After putting away our sins, He then places His life of perfect holiness in the believers' hands. He shares it with them. He imparts it to them. It is this which becomes their key to Heaven, their right to partake of the tree of life, their title deed to heavenly bliss, their beauteous dress to stand before God.

This holy life is made available to every believer. The truth of redemption lies in this: "Knowing . . . that our old man [our life before conversion] is crucified with Him, that the body of sin [something always alive] might be destroyed, that henceforth we should not serve sin" (Romans 6:6). The word "destroyed" is the same as that used in relation to our Lord's coming to destroy the devil. It is not annihilation. It means "rendered idle or unproductive." By faith we lay it aside and refuse to feed it.

By faith we live by the new life imparted to us through the presence and power of the Holy Spirit residing within us. It is not written without meaning or without truth that He "hath raised us up together, and made us sit together in heavenly places in Christ Jesus" (Ephesians 2:6). This heavenly position is for very practical purposes here on earth—that we should live under the control of the Holy Spirit and not allow sin to "reign in [our] mortal body, that [we] should obey it in the lusts thereof" (Romans 6:12). It is conquest of the flesh through the conquest by Christ our Lord.

> Out of my bondage, sorrow, and night,
> Jesus, I come, Jesus, I come;

Into Thy freedom, gladness, and light,
 Jesus, I come to Thee;
Out of my sickness into Thy health,
Out of my want and into Thy wealth,
Out of my sin and into Thyself,
 Jesus, I come to Thee.

Out of my shameful failure and loss,
 Jesus, I come, Jesus, I come;
Into the glorious gain of the cross,
 Jesus, I come to Thee;
Out of earth's sorrows into Thy balm,
Out of life's storms and into Thy calm,
Out of distress to jubilant psalm,
 Jesus, I come to Thee.

Out of the fear and dread of the tomb,
 Jesus, I come, Jesus, I come;
Into the joy and light of Thy home,
 Jesus, I come to Thee;
Out of the depth of ruin untold,
Into the peace of Thy sheltering fold,
Ever Thy glorious face to behold,
 Jesus, I come to Thee.

W. T. SLEEPER

42

THE CROSS AND THE HOLY SPIRIT

> Christ hath redeemed us from the curse of the law,
> being made a curse for us . . . That the blessing of Abraham
> might come on the Gentiles through Jesus Christ; that we
> might receive the promise of the Spirit through faith
> (Galatians 3:13-14).

You will see at once from these verses that there is a
vital connection between the cross of Christ and the gift
of the Holy Spirit. That is a relationship most profound.
Historically the cross had to come before the Holy Spirit
of the glorified Christ could be given. Sin had to be cleansed
away before the Holy Spirit could indwell man.

The Work of the Holy Spirit

The work of the Holy Spirit in creation was to bring
order out of chaos (Genesis 1:2) by His wisdom, power,
and energy—transforming a work that was waste and void
into one of beauty, harmony, and order. His work in the
history of Israel was to take the leadership of that redeemed
nation, guiding them through a trackless desert, filling and
endowing men like Bezaleel with skill and wisdom to build
the Tabernacle to a divine pattern. His work in the life of
the Lord Jesus was to prepare a body for Him in the womb
of Mary, anointing Him to speak the words and do the works
the Father assigned Him, enabling Him to offer Himself
as a sacrifice for sins. His work in the Church was to bring
it into being on the day of Pentecost, to administer its
government, to furnish it with gifts, to direct and control

154

all its operations. His work in individuals in this age is to convict of sin, to point sinners to Christ and Him crucified, and to witness in the deepest consciousness of their being that they are born of God.

The relationship between the cross of the Lord Jesus and the Holy Spirit can be seen in types—bright jewels in the Bible crown—a pleasure ground for spiritual minds—steps to ever-brightening views of divine realities. For instance, the death of the Lord Jesus is prefigured in the slain paschal lamb in Israel, and the Holy Spirit is seen in their redemption which followed, under the figure of a pillar of cloud in the day and a pillar of fire by night.

In the wilderness, the suffering Saviour is seen in the smitten rock, and the Holy Spirit in the life-giving water which gushed from that rock. In the New Testament, Christ in His death is pictured in His baptism, followed by the descent of the Holy Spirit as a dove to light upon Him. Then comes the reality of the cross followed fifty days later by the descent of the Holy Spirit on the day of Pentecost. Thus we see the cross and the Holy Spirit are always together.

The Work of the Cross

The cross removes all hindrances to the indwelling of the Holy Spirit in the life of the believer. From the cross comes a stream which cleanses from all sin. From the Saviour's wounded side flows blood which removes every offensive impediment. They are a thrice-happy people who find the value of the cross, and the more they dig into the truth of it, the richer is the ore which they find.

In Romans the cross deals with sin (Romans 3:24-25). Paul proves that both Jew and Gentile are in human ruin because of sin. But God sent forth His beloved Son to deal with the fact and issues of sin—to atone for it, to obtain eternal redemption from it. He died for us. No sufferings were counted too great to buy and purchase us as His own. He waded through all the billows of God's wrath to set us free, and to cleanse us from all stains.

In Corinthians the cross deals with selfism (1 Corinthians 2:2). Our natural heritage is a sinful self, which has a darkened mind, unclean affections, and a disobedient will. Only the cross can deal with all that mass which belongs to such a fallen nature, so that we can triumph over it.

In Galatians the cross deals with legalism (Galatians 2:19-20). "Do this!" was the requirement of the law. "Live!" was the recompense. But an imperfect man cannot keep a perfect law, for man has trampled that law beneath his feet, and scattered its promises to the winds.

In Ephesians the cross deals with earthiness (Ephesians 4:22-23). Our position is in the heavenlies with Christ, but we are often earthbound by such things as nationalism, social standing, color sensitivity, religious affiliation, possession of riches, all of which are of the earth, earthy. Only the cross can enable us to put off this old man with all its bindings.

In Philippians the cross deals with earthly gain (Philippians 3:7). In this realm Paul had much more than most men of those things which men esteem of value: birth, inheritance, upbringing, education, prestige, status. But the cross sweeps away all pride in such things, so that the Holy Spirit may possess the whole life.

In Colossians the cross deals with worldly philosophy (Colossians 2:4). The Gnostics had a philosophy about creation—about human matter being evil in itself, which issued in license to sin most grossly. This oriental mysticism was flavored a little with Mosaic ritual to give it a show of religion, but the cross swept away this refuge of lies.

In Thessalonians the cross deals with temperamental oddities (2 Thessalonians 3:11-12). There were those who, after hearing of the coming again of the Lord Jesus, gave up their work and sat around in idleness, eating other people's bread. The cross condemned this kind of life, and God's Word insists that we "occupy till He come"—to keep busy in His interest until He appears.

> In the cross of Christ I glory,
> Towering o'er the wrecks of time;

All the light of sacred story
    Gathers round its head sublime.

When the woes of life o'ertake me,
    Hopes deceive, and fears annoy,
Never shall the cross forsake me;
    Lo! it glows with peace and joy.

Bane and blessing, pain and pleasure,
    By the cross are sanctified;
Peace is there which knows no measure,
    Joys that through all time abide.

JOHN BOWRING

43

SELF-DENIAL IN THE CROSS

The Son of man must suffer . . . and be slain. . . . If
any man will come after Me, let him deny himself, and take
up his cross daily, and follow Me (Luke 9:22-23).

In this Scripture our Lord speaks for the first time
concerning His coming sufferings and death. Immediately
afterward, He speaks of those who would be His followers
taking up their cross. As a propitiatory offering, the sacrifice of our Lord was final and complete. He died unto
sins once, and Calvary is never to be repeated.

When He rose from the dead He still bore the marks
of the nails. He showed His disciples His hands and His side
(John 20:20). The material and physical aspects of the cross
were gone, but the marks were still there. They were there

to show His disciples what fellowship with Him would mean—oneness of mission, oneness of spirit, and oneness of wounds.

The cross is the only pattern for Christian discipleship. We cannot emulate the Lord in the days of His flesh. There were things He did which we cannot do. The pattern of His death is the only pattern for Christian life. We are called to be conformed to His death.

The kind of death believers and followers are involved in is not physical death—though it may include that, as martyrs can testify. But not all believers are called to be crucified on a cross as our Lord was. Nor is the death to which we are called a redemptive one. We can have no part at all in redemption, nor can we contribute the slightest thing to it. That is the mischief of the church of Rome. It denies that Jesus alone can suffice.

But no human work can be the groundwork of a sinner's hope. The sacrifice for sins was Christ's and His alone. It is an offense to God to add anything to that finished work. It is not Christ added to angels, Christ added to saints, Christ added to the church, Christ added to mediators, Christ added to human toil, Christ added to penance, or Christ added to purgatory. That is an idol of clay, and the Word of God concerning it is sure: "Christ is become of no effect unto you, whosoever of you are justified by the law; ye are fallen from grace" (Galatians 5:4).

There are two sides to the cross of the Lord Jesus Christ. One is redemptive; the other is exemplary. The Scriptures are clear that we can have no part, nor make any contribution, toward the redemptive aspect of the cross. But there is an exemplary side which we may emulate. In this aspect we gaze upon Him as our example; and, having been saved through the redemptive work of the cross, we are to imitate certain elements in that cross-work. Since we are saved wholly by His grace, we are to dedicate ourselves—our souls, our bodies, all that we are, all that we have, all that we can do—as a living sacrifice to God. We are not to keep anything from Him who has given all of Himself for us. This is what must rise from redeemed hearts, and what alone can make our offering a sweet savor unto God.

The Self-Denial in the Cross

"If any man will come after Me, let him deny himself, and take up his cross daily, and follow Me." The taking up of the cross is a figure of speech. It is not copying our Lord when the wooden cross, upon which He was crucified, was forced upon Him. We are to take up our cross daily. Whatever is involved, it is a continuous exercise, a daily thing.

Apart from the redemptive aspect, then, the cross of Jesus calls for the utmost self-denial. But taking up that wooden cross was used by our Lord as a metaphor to express this self-denial. When that cross was laid upon a man, it meant his life was forfeited—given up—surrendered to the state. He had now no rights of his own. His life was given up to another. Our Lord uses such an extreme case to show us what self-denial really is.

Self-denial is not giving up sweets, tobacco, alcohol, movies, and such things for a certain period of the year called Lent, though it may involve the surrender of such things. It is giving up our whole self to the Lord; not only laying down the burden of every sin but, having done that, and having trusted the finished work of Christ for our salvation, to offer, by the Spirit's power, the whole of a devoted and adoring life.

The example of this is our Lord in His cross—in His sufferings and death. Paul makes this clear in Philippians 2:6-8. The Lord Jesus, before His descent into the world, was existing as God over all—Sovereign Lord of all the universe. But He counted not this form of existence something to be held on to. He could change the form of His existence without ceasing to be who He was—the mighty God.

It meant, however, the surrender of certain privileges and prerogatives, the laying aside of all visible manifestations of glory, clothing Himself with the poor rags of our humanity, and existing as a servant in the likeness of men. Therefore He humbled Himself. He exchanged sovereignty for servitude. He came as the Divine Servant to do nothing but God's will. There was no compulsion—and no reluctance. His step was perfect willingness.

This is His example for Christian living. There can be no imitating our Lord in such self-denial until we are saved by the Lord through His grace and have that life of His imparted to us. It is only His life in us which can reproduce that abnegation. Thus the apostle says, "Let this mind be in you, which was also in Christ Jesus" (Philippians 2:5). There can be no such abnegation without the mind of Christ in us. With His mind, God's interests alone will be our consuming desire.

Saviour, Thy dying love
    Thou gavest me,
Nor should I aught withhold,
    Dear Lord, from Thee:
In love my soul would bow,
My heart fulfill its vow,
Some offering bring Thee now,
    Something for Thee.

Give me a faithful heart,
    Likeness to Thee,
That each departing day
    Henceforth may see
Some work of love begun,
Some deed of kindness done,
Some wanderer sought and won,
    Something for Thee.

All that I am and have—
    Thy gifts so free—
In joy, in grief, through life,
    Dear Lord, for Thee!
And when Thy face I see,
My ransomed soul shall be,
Through all eternity,
    Something for Thee.

SYLVANUS D. PHELPS

44

SELF-CONTROL IN THE CROSS

Servants, be subject to your masters with all fear; not
only to the good and gentle, but also to the froward. For
this is thankworthy, if a man for conscience toward God
endure grief, suffering wrongfully. For what glory is it, if,
when ye be buffeted for your faults, ye shall take it patiently? but if, when ye do well, and suffer for it, ye take it
patiently, this is acceptable with God. For even hereunto
were ye called: because Christ also suffered for us, leaving
us an example, that ye should follow His steps" (1 Peter
2:18-21).

This Scripture makes very clear that there is an exemplary side of the cross—a side which we are to imitate.
In His cross, the Lord Jesus has left us an example to follow. His cross is the pattern for Christian living. We cannot
walk as He walked, or in His steps as He trod the earth.
We can, however, after being saved, emulate certain elements
which He exhibited in His cross.

Exemplified by Jesus

During those days just previous to the cross, and indeed
while hanging on that cruel instrument of death, our Lord
was subjected to every kind of abuse. He was scourged until
the skin was taken off His back; the hairs of His head were
plucked out; "His visage was so marred more than any man";
He was insulted, mocked, spat on, ridiculed, taunted about
His trust in God, smitten with a reed, and crowned with
sharp thorns. All this was meted out to Him most unjustly.
To that mocking mob, He seems "a worm and no man."

Did our Lord deserve this? Of course not! He did no sin, neither was guile found in His mouth. Pilate found no fault in Him, neither could the X-rays of God's holy law find the slightest thing at which it could point an accusing finger.

Now all this He endured with patience and perfect self-control. There was in Him no thought of revenge. He did not keep a little black book to record such insults and harbor grudges. He did not think for one moment of repayment for their evil deeds. "When He suffered, He threatened not" (1 Peter 2:23). Lovers of revenge cannot dwell on this hallowed ground. If a believer desires sanctification—pants to be conformed to the image of Christ—then he must learn what self-control means, and he can learn it only at the cross of Christ our Lord.

In this Epistle Peter was writing to the believers scattered far and wide throughout Pontus, Galatia, Cappadocia, Asia, and Bithynia. In those days many believers were slaves of masters, most of whom were heathen. In the verses at the head of this chapter, Peter is counseling them about their conditions. He says, in effect, that if they are beaten for doing wrong and take it patiently, there is no glory in that! They endure it patiently because they know they deserve it for their wrongdoing.

But if they are buffeted for their Christian life and witness—that is, undeservedly and unjustly—and take that patiently, then it is something acceptable with God, because it is an image of Christ. Believers are not to take revenge. They are not to retaliate when they are wrongfully treated. They are not to be bitter and resentful.

Expected of the Believer

This, said Peter, is that to which we are called. This is Christian conduct in the face of unjust treatment. The cross reflects our Lord's true character and, in the mirror of it, we see how we should live and act. Mercy and love trace a path for their fullest exercise even under the most provocative circumstances. Our Lord's heart was in perfect repose.

Throughout these base assaults, no billow of impatience heaved within Him. No storm of angry revenge rose up in Him. We are to gaze upon Him and see in such conduct our own high calling in Him. It is not just to suffer—not just to suffer unjustly, which we may do with stoical feelings and hardened determination. No! We are to suffer patiently and without thought of revenge.

People are just the same today. Human nature has not improved with the advance of civilization. The world of unregenerate men is just as rude, unkind, mean, and hateful as at any other time in history. There are saints who have been in prison for many years in China; others have been exiled to freezing and lonely places in Russia; still others have been persecuted beyond description in Africa. Many in our own country have suffered the ribald mockery of rude men. The natural heart tends to resent such treatment, to bear a grudge, to seek opportunity for revenge, to plan retaliation.

The call for Christian living is to be conformed to our Lord Jesus Christ, to be conformed to His death, to emulate His behavior as He went to the cross of shame. In Him we see nothing but perfect self-control. If we are called to suffer unjustly, we are to do so without complaint, to do so patiently. How we stand up under suffering, and how we bear it, is not only a test of Christian character, but it reveals Christian character, and develops likeness and conformity to Christ our Lord and Saviour. There is no severer test for the Christian than how we endure unkind and unjust treatment.

Fill all my vision, Saviour, I pray,
Let me see only Jesus today;
Though through the valley Thou leadest me,
Thy fadeless glory encompasseth me.

Fill all my vision, Saviour divine,
Till with Thy glory my spirit shall shine,

Fill all my vision, that all may see
Thy holy Image reflected in me.

Fill all my vision, let naught of sin
Shadow the brightness shining within.
Let me see only Thy blessed face,
Feasting my soul on Thy infinite grace.

AVIS B. CHRISTIANSEN

45

SELF-SACRIFICE IN THE CROSS

Hereby perceive we the love of God, because He laid
down His life for us: and we ought to lay down our lives
for the brethren (1 John 3:16).

Self-sacrifice is the pouring out of life on behalf of
others. This is the high point of taking up our cross and
following our Lord. There is no compulsion in the things of
God. God never compels. The things of the Spirit are voluntary, else they have no value. We read that the Romans
"laid hold upon one Simon, a Cyrenian, coming out of
the country, and on him they laid the cross, that he might
bear it after Jesus" (Luke 23:26). The cross-bearing of
true discipleship is not so. It is born of love, and it is taken
up voluntarily. It must be pure delight—an expression of
gratitude for His redeeming love.

Our Lord's love was very practical. It came down to
where we were and met our deepest need. And this is what
we are to do in relation to others. So, after telling us what
our Lord did, John tells us that we should do the same.
He also suggests what that may imply. "Whoso hath this

world's good, and seeth his brother have need, and shutteth up his bowels of compassion from him, how dwelleth the love of God in him?" (1 John 3:17)

The implication is that when we see persons in need we are to alleviate that need. We are to give food to the hungry and shelter to the homeless. We are to befriend the friendless, care for the aged, visit the sick, extend help to the deformed and the retarded. Love has an open hand, and that hand of help must be open if we are to follow the Lord.

The liberality of God is easily seen in the lesser realm of our physical need. How lovingly and abundantly God has provided—and that for a race most undeserving. He wills, and crops abound. He speaks, and garners overflow. God's provision is an inexhaustible feast. It feeds the hungry and never fails.

But God's supreme example of giving is in the cross. When God gave His beloved Son, He gave all. Had He given all the angels in Heaven, it would have been a mighty spectacular, but would have been as dross compared to the giving of His Son. God gave His Son—not some animal, man, or angel. Moreover, He gave His Son to die the shameful death of the cross, and He gave His Son for rebellious, degenerate, and ruined man. Because of this magnanimous giving the beloved Son became our Surety and our Saviour, and through His sacrifice we are redeemed and saved with an eternal security.

We have no part in that redeeming act of God but, receiving the life of God into our souls through faith in His Son, the kindness of God becomes the chief characteristic of the life of the child of God. His children give and give and give. Their joy in salvation expresses itself in gratitude, and gratitude expresses itself in giving to those who are needy, though undeserving. These good works are the surest proof of faith. An empty hand proclaims a graceless heart. No true believer can see others perish through neglect. Christian life is a constant pouring out of self on behalf of others.

It is possible, of course, to give money, food, time, and much more, yet not give yourself. These things are not substitutes for the giving of oneself. On the other hand, you can give money, food, time, and much more as a genuine expression of self-giving. You can give yourself in your gifts.

This is what the cross meant to our Lord and Saviour. He gave Himself. He poured out His life for us. He bore our griefs and carried our sorrows. How great was His love! How dear we must be to His heart! He, who is the preciousness of Heaven, descended to serve the worst.

What can we render unto the Lord for all His benefits? We must give ourselves—our souls, our bodies, our every faculty and gift, our influence, our means, our morning, our midday, our evening hours, to be a free-will sacrifice. Our whole life must be one clear blaze of flaming love and ever-brightening service to others. This is what taking up the cross means to us. It was so with our Lord. "He humbled Himself." He emptied Himself. We must do the same. He has left us that example in the cross.

More and more, giving should be the motto of our lives. Higher and higher should be our heavenward flight. Deeper and deeper should be the stream of love. Wider and wider should be the fruit of that service. All this, not to gain salvation, but as an expression of our gratitude for salvation, and as an exhibition of the kindness and goodness of the life of Christ within us.

> What grace, O Lord, and beauty shone
> Around Thy steps below!
> What patient love was seen in all
> Thy life and death of woe!
>
> Oh, give us hearts to love like Thee—
> Like Thee, O Lord, to grieve
> Far more for others' sins than all
> The wrongs that we receive.
>
> One with Thyself, may every eye
> In us, Thy brethren, see

That gentleness and grace that spring
From union, Lord, with Thee.

EDWARD DENNY

46

MELCHIZEDEK'S BLESSING

Melchizedek king of Salem brought forth bread and
wine: and he was the priest of the most high God (Genesis
14:18).

Thou art a priest for ever after the order of Melchisedec" (Hebrews 5:6).

This is a marvelous, wondrous scene. Abraham is moving
toward home after a great victory and is laden with spoil.
Suddenly, a strange person meets him in the way. He is
both a priest and a king. But his lineage none can tell. His
descent is hid from our eyes so that it can be said of him,
"Without father, without mother, without descent, having
neither beginning of days, nor end of life" (Hebrews 7:3).
Thus he is made a special type of our Lord, who is, by
eternal generation, the coequal Son of the coequal Father—
God of God, and very God of very God. That is too deep for
finite minds. We would have to have God's mind to understand God's essence, and to have His infinitude to understand His nature. From eternity past to eternity to come,
our Lord's being is never other than the eternal Son of
God.

King of Righteousness

In being king of righteousness, Melchizedek is but a type, for none can claim that title but the Son of God. Since Adam fell, this earth has seen no righteous man apart from the Lord Jesus. So we learn that, first of all, the Lord's kingdom is one of righteousness (Romans 4:17). His throne is pure white in righteousness. Every statute, decree, ordinance, commandment, precept, reward, and penalty, is altogether righteous.

King of Peace

Melchizedek's city was Salem, meaning "peace." There may have been wars and quarrels outside, but within the gates of Salem all was peace and quietness. Here again Melchizedek stands as a type of the Lord Jesus, whose kingdom is a realm of peace.

Those who belong to that kingdom have surrendered their arms of rebellion. There is no more enmity. Our Lord has changed the heart of stone into a warm heart of filial love. The delight of His subjects is to walk by His side, to listen to His voice, to sing His praise. There is no peace save in Jesus' kingdom of Salem.

Priest of the Most High God

So Melchizedek was consecrated to stand before God and thus to exhibit Christ in His function as Priest of His people. Christ is our Altar, for only He could bear the load of human transgression. He is also our Sacrifice upon the altar, and in this office He is the Lamb of God to make a full and sufficient sacrifice for sins.

But He is also our Priest, who can draw nigh to God on our behalf and offer His own blood within the veil. Having obtained eternal redemption, He has entered the holiest of all with His own blood; in doing so, He has abolished all our need for other priests, other sacrifices, other altars here on earth. His work below is finished.

He, however, lives as our High Priest above forever, and there He sits on the right hand of the Majesty on high. The voice of His intercession prevails. We are blessed because of His prayers. Our offerings of worship, adoration, prayer, praise, thanksgiving, and service, are all perfumed with His adorable merits. All are made worthy in His worthiness.

Food for the Believer

"Melchizedek . . . brought forth bread and wine." At this time, Abraham was returning from battle and was faint and weary. But Melchizedek met him, and the anointed priest refreshed Abraham with bread and wine. Here again we see Jesus in figure—our great High Priest on high making provision to renew our wasted strength, to lift up our drooping spirits, to revive our fainting hearts. What can this point to but the memorial feast which was left us by the Lord Jesus, and which is His provision for His people's needs.

The fight of faith is fierce. The journey of life is sometimes long and very arduous. But the Lord has opened His banqueting house along the way and spread His feast. There is no greater refreshment for the saints of God than to come to this feast and feed upon the bread and wine. These are but tokens of what He is in Himself, a spiritual feast and food abundant, His own body given, His own blood shed. Jesus is the true Melchizedek and comes forth to meet us in life's way. While we sit at His banqueting table and regale our souls by feasting upon Him, we hear Him say what I believe was said to Abraham: "Blessed be thou of the most high God."

In gratitude for this bounty, the patriarch of old, Abraham, made an offering of the tenth part of all to Melchizedek. When we come to the Lord's remembrance feast, the bread is a whole loaf, the cup is full, the money bag is empty. But the bread is eaten; the cup is drunk; and then, in gratitude, the bag is filled with the offerings of

His people. Let us not suppose such offerings to be a compulsory obedience to law. They are, for believers, the expressions of their gratitude that, through our Lord's redeeming love, they have come within His kingdom of righteousness and peace—bought by precious blood, drawn by melting grace, called by His constraining voice.

> The atoning work is done,
>   The Victim's blood is shed;
> And Jesus now has gone
>   His people's cause to plead:
> He stands in Heaven, their great High Priest,
> And bears their names upon His breast.
>
> No temple made with hands
>   His place of service is;
> In Heaven itself He stands,
>   A heavenly priesthood His:
> In Him the shadows of the law
> Are all fulfilled, and now withdrawn.
>
> And though awhile He be
>   Hid from the eyes of men,
> His people look to see,
>   Their great High Priest again:
> In brightest glory He will come
> And take His waiting people home.
>
> THOMAS KELLY

47

A LITTLE WHILE

> For yet a little while, and the wicked shall not be:
> yea, thou shalt diligently consider his place, and it shall
> not be (Psalm 37:10).

> A little while, and ye shall not see Me: and again,
> a little while, and ye shall see Me, because I go to the
> Father (John 16:16).

> For yet a little while, and He that shall come will
> come, and will not tarry (Hebrews 10:37).

It is evident from John 16:16 that, during our Lord's discourse in the upper room prior to His death, His disciples did not understand Him. Spiritual things were slow to penetrate their mind. Our Lord's two references to "a little while" baffled them: "A little while, and ye shall not see Me: and again, a little while, and ye shall see Me."

The Reference to His Death

The reference of the first part of the verse was to His death. About His death the Lord added: "Ye shall weep and lament, but the world shall rejoice" (John 16:20). It would be a time of great sorrow for His own. It would mean the loss of His personal physical presence. They were wont to fly to Him in moments of difficulty, to resort to Him in moments of perplexity, and to go to Him with their questions. Now He was going from them, and their hearts were heavy at the thought of His departure. The rock of their confidence, the delight of their eyes, the hope of their souls was to be taken from them. They would be left like orphans. They had left all for Him. Now He was leaving them.

It meant also the disappointment of their earthly hopes. They had been looking for an earthly kingdom. They believed the Roman yoke would be taken off. Israel would again be the chiefest of the nations. But without Him these hopes now began to vanish. There would be no kingdom on earth. So they thought, and, with the dashing of their hopes, they would weep and lament.

It meant also that they would witness His agonies. They would see Him falsely accused, insulted by menials, reviled by abjects, forsaken by friends, scorned and ridiculed by enemies. They would have to listen to the derision of the mad crowd. They would have to hear His cry as He became forsaken even of God.

It also exposed them to become the butt of the world's ridicule. "The world [would] rejoice" to see Jesus bearing His cross. The world would rejoice that His influence was at an end, that soon He would speak no more. Nothing hurts so much in sorrow as the coarse laughter of adversaries. So His disciples would weep and lament—and within twelve hours it was to be so—"a little while" indeed! The only two bright spots in His death and burial were to be Joseph, who provided a place for His body, and Nicodemus, who provided perfume to anoint that body.

The Reference to His Resurrection

"And again, a little while" (three days in fact) "and ye shall see Me." This was a reference to His resurrection. It would have this effect on His disciples: "Your sorrow shall be turned into joy. . . . Your heart shall rejoice, and your joy no man taketh from you" (John 16:20,22). He would rise from the dead, spend forty days with them before His ascension into Heaven, and fit them for their future task by sending the Holy Spirit to reside within them.

The cause of their sorrow—His death—would become

the source of their joy as they would learn the value of the redemption purchased. His resurrection would assure them of that! The greatest possible blessings would accrue from His resurrection. Their sorrow would be turned into lasting joy. Their hearts would sing; their hopes revive.

Blessings untold would come to them. An inheritance in Heaven, incorruptible and undefiled, would be procured for them. He would see them again and would give them the deepest certitude of which the human consciousness is capable; He would bring this about by His appearances to them after His resurrection.

The Reference to His Coming Again

"For yet a little while, and He that shall come will come, and will not tarry" (Hebrews 10:37). The Hebrew believers, to whom the apostle was writing, were suffering under persecution. Trials are necessary if faith is to be found to God's praise and honor. A vessel may have the appearance of gold, but a bit of scouring may show the gold to be only surface painting. Hirelings cannot stand scouring. They become changelings under trial.

"Yet a little while"—just a little while in God's reckoning, and a little while in comparison to the endless ages when believers will be with the Lord forever. We are prone to compare time with time, but God compares time with eternity, and makes it a very small thing indeed! Lest some lament and ask: "Why tarriest Thou, O Lord?" He tells us that He will not tarry—not a single hour beyond what time is necessary to fulfill His purposes.

Soon, soon, believers shall raise triumphant songs. Soon we shall wave our verdant wands. Soon shall we cry our hosannas: "Blessed is He that cometh." Oh, how we shall joy in final victory, in palm-waving ecstasy, in singing salvation's hymn: "Unto Him that loved us, and washed us from our sins in His own blood" (Revelation 1:5). When the Lord Jesus comes, no distance shall intervene again—no separation again occur!

The Reference to the Judgment of the Wicked

"For yet a little while, and the wicked shall not be" (Psalm 37:10). The wicked are a vile mass. There is no refuge to protect them. None shall break their chains. God is their adversary. God's holiness must heat the furnace of His wrath. Death is to plunge them in a deep, deep woe, and eternity usher them into hell. How sad!

> O child of God, there is for thee
> A hope that shines amidst the gloom,
> A gladsome hope that thou shalt see
> Thy Lord, for He will surely come.
>
> He'll come, yes, He'll come and tarry not;
> He'll come, yes, He'll come and tarry not;
> He'll come, He'll come, He'll come and tarry not.
>
> Then joy unmingled will be thine,
> Earth's tears and trials all forgot;
> So cheer thy heart, no more repine,
> His word is sure: "He'll tarry not."

T. D. W. MUIR

48

FORERUNNER INTO THE HOLIEST

Whither the forerunner is for us entered, even Jesus, made an high priest for ever after the order of Melchisedec (Hebrews 6:20).

Our Lord Jesus Christ is for us a Forerunner entered into Heaven. We do not hear much of this, but it is vitally important. It really should read "a forerunner," not "the forerunner." The latter could refer back to a type, but there is no such type in the Old Testament. The idea of our Lord's being a forerunner into the actual presence of God was something entirely foreign to the Hebrew mind. Let us be clear what such an office means.

A Representative

Our Lord entered Heaven as Representative of a people who were to follow Him there. Notice that in the title verse only the human name of Jesus is emphasized, for He entered in as the Son of man. It was never true that any Jewish high priest was a forerunner. True, these men went into the holy of holies in the Tabernacle once a year on the day of atonement, but never as forerunners—for the people of Israel as a nation could never follow them into that very holy place. Israel has no such hope.

The Lord Jesus did just that! Having made sacrifice for sins with His own precious blood, He entered into the holiest in Heaven—into the real presence of God—and did so as the Son of man. Spiritually, those who are in Christ by new birth may enter in at this present time, and enjoy fellowship and communion with the Father and the Son through the Spirit. But the thought expressed in Hebrews 6 is that of entering in all the fullness of our manhood, which means, as it did for our Lord, in a resurrection body.

Such is the lesson which this solemnity directly gives us. This is to gain much more than Adam lost. By His redemption, the Lord Jesus gains for us a heavenly inheritance. He purposes to establish us in much more than an Eden heritage. He goes before to a land of peace, where God shall be our very present God and our loving Father forever. Here is found, then, much more than was ever lost through sin. We have a sure estate. The Lord is our Representative so that we shall enter in where He is. Where He is, and all that He is, and all that He has, is ours.

A Guarantor

First of all, He is a Guarantor to God, taking responsibility that our presence there will not defile God's holy Heaven. His presence within the veil is also a guarantee to us that we shall never be expelled. The context of Hebrews 6:20 shows that the apostle has been reminding the Hebrew Christians of a day when they fled for refuge to lay hold of the hope set before them in Jesus the Lord. In Old Testament days the case was possible, that man, without intent, without one evil revengeful thought, might stain his hands in human blood. The kinsman of the man slain could rise up in wrath and claim the slayer's life. The law gave license to take blood for blood. So for the slayer, peace and security fled forever. He would be afraid in any place. But Israel's God provided a rescue to such lasting woe. He gave cities of refuge for security, and the death of the high priest dissolved all avenging claims. The slayer was free when the high priest died. He could go forth unmolested.

The apostle was setting before these disturbed Hebrew Christians the security they have in Christ. What was their hope in so fleeing to Jesus? The answer—a security of life which gave them "a strong consolation." That consolation was based on two immutable things: God's word and God's oath. This hope, therefore, became "as an anchor of the soul, both sure and steadfast, and which entereth into that within the veil" (Hebrews 6:18-19). No image could be more beautiful and consoling. The sureness and steadfastness of an anchor depends upon its catching hold of something immovable. It will then hold a ship no matter what storm is raging.

So, we are told, is the believer's hope in the Lord Jesus Christ. The world is a troubled sea. But let the tempest rage and howl, let the tide run ever so strong against us, our little ships will never drift on rock and make wreck of us. We shall never perish. He who is the Messenger of the New Covenant—our Surety—our Mediator—has entered into Heaven already. We have a joining chain with Him. He it is who guarantees to hold us fast and bring us safely home to glory. What a cordial to the faint-hearted, a haven for the tempted, a kerchief for weeping eyes, a pillow for the doubting!

A Preparer

"In My Father's house. . . . I go to prepare a place for you" (John 14:2). Our place has been prepared from the moment our Lord entered Heaven. We are not to think in terms of material construction as though our Lord were erecting something. The Father's house has always been there. Our Forerunner, Jesus, entered to make Heaven ready for us, and works in us to make us ready for Heaven. We do not need a key. The door has been opened by our Saviour's triumphal ascension, and He has left the door open for all who believe to follow Him.

When Israel journeyed in the wilderness, the ark of the Lord went three days' journey before them to prepare a settlement. So our Lord, by His resurrection and ascension, has gone to prepare a place for us. Therefore, He says, "Let not your heart be troubled: ye believe in God, believe also in Me" (John 14:1). The consolation of believers cannot spring from earth. The claims of this world are worthless. Earthly toys are worse than empty bubbles. The world has nothing to give the believer.

"In the world ye shall have tribulation" (John 16:33). Affliction may break upon us like a ceaseless tide. This is to be expected. It is our common lot. Sorrow will find a door to each of us, but the Lord enters along with it to support the believer in the way. "Time is short." Sorrow is not forever. "Let not your heart be troubled."

We have a home to go to in the Heaven of heavens. So we have to meet terminal sickness and then go through the dark valley? But we do not go alone and it is only "the valley of the shadow of death"—that is, only the shadow of it will fall upon us. The Lord Jesus has said: "I am with you," and He will guide us safely through to the prepared home with its many mansions. Everything is fully prepared. He has done all things well.

> By faith I look where Christ has gone,
> And see upon His Father's throne
>   A Man, with glory crowned.
> His brow is marred, and on His side,
> Whence flowed the cleansing crimson tide,
>   The marks of love are found.
>
> I look again, and now I see
> That blessed Man engaged for me,
>   His hands uplifted high;
> Before the throne of God He pleads,
> God's great High Priest, He intercedes,
>   And so preserves me nigh.
>
> What love! He washed my sins away,
> Thus boldness in the Judgment Day
>   For me there doth remain.
> What grace! now occupied with me,
> He wills I should His glory see,
>   When He returns again!

                    C. E. PEGLAR

49

THE REIGNING LAMB

And I beheld, and, lo, in the midst of the throne and
of the four beasts, and in the midst of the elders, stood
a Lamb as it had been slain (Revelation 5:6).

The Lamb in the midst is central to the whole revelation of God. Here is one of the most thrilling and exciting
chapters in Holy Writ. Our Lord's humiliation is past; His
exaltation is present. He is high and lifted up, as Isaiah
promised He would be. The scene is one of magnificence
and majesty, and there is nothing to equal it as a grand
spectacular.

The Triumph of the Lamb

At the center of the vision is a rainbow-encircled throne
on which the Lord God is seated with a seven-sealed book
in His hand. Seven being the number of completion, it
represents a completely sealed book. It is not a book of the
past, nor of the present, but of the future. It has to do with
the finalities of human history, the winding up of this old
creation, the final fulfillment of God's purposes, the ultimate issues of human destiny, the bringing in of a new
Heaven and a new earth.

A challenge is put forth by a strong angel as to who
is worthy to open the book and to loose the seals. John
weeps much because no man of Adam's race could open,
read, or even look upon such a book. He is told, however,
to cease weeping, for the Lion of the tribe of Judah has
prevailed to do so. When John turns to see the Lion, he

179

sees instead a Lamb—a newly slain little Lamb. The Lord Jesus prevailed over all opposing forces as a strong Lion, but He did so as the Lamb of God in the blood-letting of the cross. That is where the victory was won.

He alone is counted worthy to open the book, and that for several reasons. He is the only One who has conquered Satan and all the hosts of hell. In His cross, the Lord stripped Satan of his weapons so that never again dare Satan come near Him, or rule over those who are sheltered in Christ. The Lord disarmed, discarded, and destroyed the devil's power. Again, the Lord Jesus is the sole Redeemer of sinful man by reason of His sufficient sacrifice for sins made on Calvary's cross. Our sins were a mighty load, but He bore and sustained them. Justice made tremendous claims upon us, but Jesus paid it all on our behalf.

The Characteristics of the Lamb

We see from Revelation 3:21 that the Son of God in His glorified humanity is seated with the Father on His throne and, as Daniel said, "the heavens do rule" (Daniel 4:26). This is a great comfort to the Lord's people who still dwell on earth amidst increasing moral breakdown, unashamed iniquity, and unblushing sexualism. The Lord reigns. The crucified Substitute for sinful man is the now-crowned sovereign Lord of all.

In Revelation 5 John describes Him in seven characteristics—four of them having to do with His human nature, and three with His divine:

(1) The Lion of Juda (verse 5), suggesting the Father's appointed King from the royal tribe of Judah, David's Son after the flesh—David, who, in the defeat of great Goliath, foreshadowed Christ's victory over Satan.

(2) The Root of David (verse 5), having the same basic office as David, a Shepherd King. One of the loveliest verses concerning our Lord's office as Shepherd is Isaiah 40:11: "He shall feed His flock like a shepherd: He shall gather the lambs with His arm, and carry them in His bosom, and shall

gently lead those that are with young."

(3) The Lamb slain (Revelation 5:6), His death, the only ransom price, the one atonement for all sin. He is not spared so that we may be redeemed.

(4) The Worthy One (verse 9), the glory of His people, the perfect Man, the ideal Man made worthy by the glory of pure sinlessness.

(5) Having seven horns (verse 6), complete power and authority. This is the exclusive divine attribute of omnipotence—absolute power in every realm of the universe.

(6) Having seven eyes (verse 6), complete perception and vision. This is the exclusive divine attribute of omniscience—absolute knowledge of all things.

(7) Having seven Spirits (verse 6), complete control and rule over all events and all created beings in every place in the universe. This is the exclusive, divine attribute of omnipresence—absolute presence in every place possible.

He is the Lord. He is God—the only begotten Son of God Most High. Being appointed by the Father to execute the work of redemption, He became Man—one of the human family by birth, bone of our bone and flesh of our flesh, very God yet truly Man. Oh, such a One! All the heavens now chant His praise, and the redeemed sing a new song: "Thou art worthy to take the book, and to open the seals thereof: for Thou wast slain, and hast redeemed us to God by Thy blood out of every kindred, and tongue, and people, and nation" (Revelation 5:9).

The Praise of the Lamb

Here is worship, adoration, praise, and thanksgiving to the Lamb by all who are in Heaven. It is again sevenfold—representing a complete ascription of praise. The Lamb in the midst of the throne is their delight; and in this happy land, this Heaven of heavens, God is their God forever and ever. Praise cries aloud to adore the Lamb. The whole being of every redeemed person reposes in an atmosphere of joy and gladness.

Billions of heavenly beings have this to say of our dear Saviour: "Worthy is the Lamb that was slain to receive power, and riches, and wisdom, and strength, and honour, and glory, and blessing" (Revelation 5:12). He only is fit to handle these things. See what takes place when sinful man grasps them! What cruelties are inflicted upon humanity— what ravishing of countries, what destruction of homes, what sorrows to people, what dark confusion, what floundering in the midst of conceit! Sinful man cannot handle these things without some vile abuse of the trust. There is only One who is worthy, and all Heaven speaks His praise— the Lamb in the midst of the throne.

Rejoice, the Lord is King!
    Your Lord and King adore,
Mortals, give thanks and sing,
    And triumph evermore:
Lift up your heart, lift up your voice!
Rejoice, again I say, rejoice!

Jesus, the Saviour, reigns,
    The God of truth and love;
When He had purged our stains,
    He took His seat above:
Lift up your heart, lift up your voice!
Rejoice, again I say, rejoice!

CHARLES WESLEY

50

THE LAMB IN THE ETERNAL CITY

The Lamb is the light thereof (Revelation 21:23).

The last two chapters of the Holy Bible are the consummation of divine revelation. The Apostle John is carried by the Spirit to a great high mountain—symbolic of spiritual elevation—that he may behold this grand and glorious vision.

The Holy City

"The holy city, new Jerusalem" seems to be both the eternal residence of the saints and also figurative of the redeemed people themselves. As a place of residence it is a holy city. Nothing can enter which defiles. There can be no tempting circumstance, no slippery path, no place, or book, or trade, or being which can draw the redeemed away from God. It is a heavenly city, "coming down from God out of heaven" (Revelation 21:2)—the epitome of supreme happiness, having "no more death, neither sorrow, nor crying, neither . . . any more pain" (Revelation 21:4), and "no night there." The name Jerusalem means "the foundation of peace"—a most comforting title for the Lord's people after the sorrows of earth.

All that the holy city is in itself is also symbolical of what the redeemed of the Lord are in themselves—a holy people with a holy citizenship, and now in the realm of supreme happiness under the benign and gracious rule of God.

The wall was "great and high" (Revelation 21:12)—

speaking of security—not as Eden which had no wall, and so was open for the tempter to lay his snare. The twelve gates were guarded by twelve angels, and written on the gates were "the names of the twelve tribes of the children of Israel" (verse 12)—indicating that God's message came through that nation which, under the severity of the law, preserved the revelation of God given to them. The twelve foundations had on them "the names of the twelve apostles of the Lamb" (verse 14)—showing us that these men laid the foundation by Spirit-inspired, apostolic teaching.

Within the city was "the river of water of life" (22:1), indicating life without pollution or corruption—a flow of divine life making for fertility, growth, and every form of beauty. "The street of it" was single, having no bypaths where one might lose his way or go astray—one way taking us ever onward into fuller revelations of the great God our Saviour. "The tree of life" in the midst—having no rival tree as in Eden, since the rebellion that the tree of the knowledge of good and evil represented had been finally dealt with, and all rebellious angels and men had been cast into the lake of fire. Each part of the city reflected some aspective portrayal of Christ, for Christ is all in all.

The Centrality of the Lamb

The Lamb is mentioned seven times in these final two chapters of Revelation. The magnificent beauty of the city, and the sublimest vision of it, is that of the Lamb within it. These seven mentions of our Lord as the Lamb in the midst of the fair city are:

(1) 21:9-10 uses the figure of the city to describe the bride of the Lamb in all her resurrection glory—the Lamb's wife.

(2) 21:14 speaks of the apostles of the Lamb, who taught the world the gospel of His grace by the inspiration of the Holy Spirit.

(3) 21:22 tells us that "the Lord God Almighty and the Lamb are the temple of it"—the city having no need of

a local temple to escape a hostile world or unsuitable weather. God and His beloved are everywhere present and occupy the whole of it.

(4) 21:23 records that "the Lamb is the light thereof"—being, as it were, the Lampholder through which the whole glory of God shines to lighten the city.

(5) 21:27 mentions "the Lamb's book of life"—without one's name written therein, one cannot enter.

(6) and (7) 22:1,3 reveal "the throne of God and of the Lamb" in it—meaning all rule and authority.

This is the consummation of the Lord's redeeming work. He is central—not only to all the prophecy and history of the past, but central to our gathering unto Him in Heaven—central to all which belongs to us in the eternal future. We shall see His face and serve Him forever.

The Closing Appeal of the Lamb

Here our little book of meditations comes to an end. It is fitting that it ends with the final message of the Lamb. They are words of solemn weight. They are the Lamb's farewell message to mankind on the pages of Holy Scripture. This is an appeal which His own remembrance feast constantly proclaims.

"Behold, I come quickly" (22:7). "Surely I come quickly" (22:20); that is, I who once came, come again. We, therefore, as believers, are to look not for some great catastrophe, terrible or glorious, for revolutions and wars, for famines and earthquakes, but for Him who said, "I come."

Before that final word, there is yet another word of appeal to all outside the Saviour. The glory of the Book of God is the revelation of God's great love. The Son reveals the Father's heart. The Gift proclaims the Giver. God's loving mercy is laid out in redemption's plan. He called His beloved Son to bear the sinner's sins. He laid all help upon a mighty Helper. It is all a signal proof of God's desire to save and bless. In a final appeal to break down ignorance, to dispel mists, to open out the way of saving grace, it is written: "And the Spirit and the bride say, Come. And let him that heareth say, Come. And let him that is athirst come. And whosoever will, let him take the water of life freely" (22:17).

Throughout the whole of Scripture, God the Holy Spirit has but one grand design—to set forth Christ the Lord before men. Sometimes this is in figures and types, which are profusely given, sometimes in skillfully constructed words, parables, miracles, and doctrines. It is all written to display the glories of Christ our Lord.

Oh, may our eyes see, our hands grasp, our feet follow, our hearts love, and our souls trust the Saviour sent by God!

"Worthy the Lamb enthroned on high,
To be exalted thus!"
"Worthy the Lamb that died!" we cry
"For He was slain for us!"

Soon shall the saints exalted high,
A glorious anthem raise;
And all that dwell below the sky
Speak forth Thine endless praise.

Redeemed creation join in one,
To praise the sacred name
Of Him that sits upon the throne,
And to exalt the Lamb.

ISAAC WATTS